Foreword

I consider it a privilege and pleasure to write the foreword to such a powerful and delightful book. Caterpillars to Butterflies sums up the beauty and the wisdom that is found within these pages.

I highly recommend that you not simply read the words, but that you also allow them to renew and set you free from any past hurts, bondage or addictions that may be limiting you from being all that you can be.

Evelyn Diment and her ministry are a beautiful and vivid illustration of what Christ desires to do in each person's life --- that they might soar on the wings of an adventure of wholeness in Him.

Pastor Ted Roberts
East Hill Church
Gresham, Oregon

TABLE OF CONTENTS

A Message from Evelyn:

This book, which started out to be a handbook on how to minister to people with addictions and people who need the healing touch of the Lord Jesus Christ, seems to be getting bigger and bigger. I feel it only fair for me to explain how I came by this information, apart from reading books, listening to tapes and hearing God from myself.

My father, who I dearly loved, had a drinking problem, which caused much heartache and turmoil in our family. When I was fourteen, shortly after my father died, I stopped trying to cope with life and blamed it on God. From then on, as I tried to find happiness in a man and failed over and over, I kept blaming God for all my wrong choices. By the time I was 50, I was a hopeless alcoholic trying to find relief in a bottle. It really surprised me to find out that I myself had become a far worse drinker than my Dad and bigger nag than my Mom, especially since I had made a solemn vow in my childhood that I'd never be like either one of them! Another thing that didn't help was my low self-esteem that began over an incident in the first grade, about a dress my Mom made for me. Little did I know that the girl who made fun of my dress would become one of the women my handsome husband would have an affair with. She was superseded by my "best friend" who beat her to the punch --- so you can see my life was off to a good start! At the age of 20, with my first born, Judy, I was on my own --- betrayed, rejected and needless to say, angry, hurt and very bitter.

One day, sitting in front of a TV with my cocktail, I happened on to the "Good News" program with Demos Shakarian, who was interviewing people God had set free from all kinds of addictions. At first I scoffed, but after two and a half hours of listening to their stories, I suddenly realized my glass was empty. As usual, when I waited too long between drinks, my body was alive with pain, nausea, the shakes, and my head was beginning to pound. I ran to the kitchen with only one thought in mind --- mix a BIG ONE --- to get my body under control again. I was astounded to hear myself say, "God, if you're real and really did deliver those people, if you would do it for me, I'll serve you!" I had no idea what serving God meant, but as I made this incredible statement, it was as if something came over me and my arm went up in the air vodka bottle and all, and down the sink went my "life support"! Right behind it came a sense of well-being, and I suddenly realized my stomach was no longer sick, my shakes had stopped, my head was no longer throbbing and the pain was gone! What a glorious, wonderful Heavenly Father we have!

4

In moments I was made whole --- my physical body as well. From then on it was as if I had never drunk --- no withdrawals or D.T.'s. You can see why my whole life now is spent sharing this glorious news and watching my Jesus heal, deliver and restore lives everywhere!

The prayers in this book are for everyone --- not just the addicted, but any believer, new or long-standing, who is still bothered by old habits and feelings that cannot be shaken and which prevent the fullness of joy the new birth stands for. When you have finished these pages, I can promise you --- "Old things will pass away and all things will be new."

Be brave--- have an exciting adventure with Jesus!

~~~~~~

Message from Rev Denise Beard 09/19/2015

** On January 20,2014 Evelyn passed from this earth at the age of 89 years old, leaving a legacy of freedom in Christ. It is my honor to carry on this work as the leader of Lively Hope Ministries. LLC.

It was with instruction of Evelyn and the support her family to transfer all rights and responsibilities of the ministry to me and that this book be re-edited and republished with scripture translated to ESV (English Standard Version).

Lively Hope continues to hold Breakthrough Seminars in the Portland, OR /Vancouver, WA area. This book is alive with the word of God and continues to lead people through to realize healing and spiritual bondage.

You can find us at: www.livelyhope.org

My heart echoes the heart of Evelyn~ I am blessed, I hope you are too.

Ephesians 3:14-19 (ESV)
Prayer for Spiritual Strength

14 For this reason I bow my knees before the Father, 15 from whom every family[a] in heaven and on earth is named, 16 that according to the riches of his glory he may grant you to be strengthened with power through his Spirit in your inner being, 17 so that Christ may dwell in your hearts through faith— that you, being rooted and grounded in love, 18 may have strength to comprehend with all the saints what is the breadth and length and height and depth, 19 and to know the love of Christ that surpasses knowledge, that you may be filled with all the fullness of God.

People with Addictions

People with addictions or chemical dependency are not just undergoing physical problems. Most treatment centers have called alcoholism a disease and alcoholics incurably ill. I certainly agree that they have physical problems, but they were caused by the alcohol and drugs after a long period of abuse; as was my physical body at the end. I was in the "pink" of health in the beginning. Their approach to helping the person control their habit is to focus on the biochemical imbalance caused by alcohol or drug abuse. They feel if they can successfully bring the body back into chemical balance, there will be no craving.

This approach ignores the spiritual and emotional side of the subject. Each part of our humanness affects the others; none is self-contained and separate. Any treatment approach that ignores parts of total well-being will not be effective in freeing people of their addictions.

The fact that they have no craving will not solve the inner turmoil that brought on the addiction (if that was how they became addicted, for there are many ways to become an addict). Even if no craving exists, they will go back to their habit, if they haven't learned how to face the pressures of this life or cope with the problems that caused them to drink or use.

Another approach is to build up the will and emotional well-being by encouragement and support of others who have struggled with drugs and alcohol. Their dependence on the group they belong to determines how well they do. Most of them admit that even though they have been dry for many months, or even years, it is always a struggle with temptation, and they are still in prison of sorts.

Most of these groups don't go far enough. They acknowledge a "hidden power", but leave it up to the person to determine who that "higher power" might be. As Christians, we realize that only a personal God, the God who lives in us, has any real power to set us free, and His name is Jesus Christ of Nazareth.

Even though people become addicted and chemically imbalanced, there are other ways people become enslaved.

1. By inheritance - generation curses and weaknesses.
2. By decision - going along with the crowd --
   a. Body rejects it at first, get sick.
   b. Body finally accepts it, stops being sick
   c. Body requires it now---demands it---can't function without it---Chemical Dependency.
3. One who has now become chemically dependent now has a diseased liver, a diseased pancreas, a pickled brain, etc. This condition is a result of the addiction, not the cause of it!!!

Proverbs 5:22,23: "The evil deeds of a wicked man ensnare (trap) him; the cords of his sin hold him fast. He will die for lack of discipline (instruction), led astray by his own great folly."

How did he become addicted?
(1) It was his using that trapped him.
(2) He was set up by wrong thinking (live like the world it's OK) and wrong living.
(3) He became trapped, held in bondage.
(4) He will die (alcohol and drugs end up killing their victims) without instruction and discipline.
(5) He would be a fool to continue following his own ways when there is help available.

Back in the beginning, in the garden, Satan sold Adam and Eve a bill of goods and got them hooked on drugs. He convinced them that there was a void in their lives, which God was holding out on them. He lied to them, telling them how great life would be if they ate from the tree. They bought the lie. They believed they would be like God, think like Him, be powerful like Him, and they acted on that lie. Suddenly they felt condemned and hid from God. They didn't feel worthy of Him.

When man steps outside God's will for his life and provision to fulfill himself by acting on a lie, he starts the addiction cycle. First he feels a void in his life; then he believes the lie, (that a drink will fix it). Then he acts on the lie (and goes to the bar); now he feels condemned. Self-hate (he has promised himself to stop so many times, he hates himself) causes him to feel empty (void), which leads to his rationalization that because he feels so bad (empty) he will use "one more time," because he needs a fix now so he can feel better. This leads to "feeling terrible" about himself, which starts the cycle all over again. And so it goes, with the hole getting deeper and the spirit of bondage now holding tighter. He now has no control on his personal life. He is controlled by alcohol and drugs.

But...there is great news!

Jesus Christ came to set us FREE.

He came to preach the Good News.

He came to bind up the brokenhearted.

He came to release the prisoners.

There is a total path to freedom, but the people who need that freedom have their part to play in it also. Nobody is an exception. There is one way to freedom and it is accomplished by total surrender on the part of the addicted and a firm grasping of the hand of Jesus. They have to leave it all behind, hold on to nothing of the past, put their trust in Him.

Coming to our "Freedom Now Group" is not like any group they have attended until now! Believe me, if you could hear their stories---of the treatment centers they have been through, the groups they have attended, the detox centers they have been in, voluntary or not---it would curl you hair. The one thing they all say that always thrills me is, "How can anything so simple be so wonderful!" None of them came expecting it to happen. They thought it was just another thing to try, perhaps to please a mate or parole officer. But WOW! When Jesus gets a hold of your life, things happen! People get completely set free of the bondage, marriages are restored, lives saved (some were on death's door like I was). I could go on and on; in fact, this might be a good time to read a few testimonies. (See Appendix)

Now all this sounds wonderful, and it is. But it was only accomplished by the following principles. Until they become strong in the Lord and the power of His might, we require a few things of the people:

1)Without truthfulness, they will go back to chemicals. Denial of their problems got them into addiction, and absolute truthfulness to God, themselves and others shuts the door to the devil. It breaks the cycle of denial, use, guilt and self-hate. The first piece of armor they put on is the belt of truth (Eph. 6)--the truth that sets them free.

2)Without accountability to someone else, they will go back to drugs and alcohol. Secrecy and independence are their worst enemies. Forming an interdependent family that cares for each other is the only way to keep the past from creeping back; otherwise, they will suddenly find themselves repeating old patterns---even though they don't want to. A new lifestyle with new friends will help break these patterns.

3) Without commitment to class attendance and the love, fellowship and understanding the group, they will go back to drugs and alcohol. The group support helps them to:

a. Break the "old ties". If they keep hanging around places and people who are using, sooner or later they will fall!!! If they don't "put off" the old life, the drugs that went with it will come up and "bite" them on the heel again!

b. Take on a new identity. Some people never break free of their past, because they are always talking about them! There is nothing funny about the "old self" and the things they did in the past. They caused them and a lot of other people a lot of misery! If they joke or take secret pride in how bad they were, they are heading for a fall---they will go back to it. They need to see that their "new identity" is what God is making them into-actually who they were meant to be before they got detoured. They need to be taught how to take pride in imitating the Heavenly Father.

c. Deal with roots of bitterness and rejection in their lives. They need to deal with the root cause of their addiction---with inner turmoil---and get healed from the inside out, or they will eventually find something to soothe the pain again.

Getting to the root gets that sliver out that kept festering and kept them from being made whole.

d. Be filled with the Word of God and the Holy Spirit. To be delivered only is not the full answer, but it allows people, without pressure from the Devil and a controlling spirit of bondage, to do their own thinking---without torment. So as we have them get rid of something we have them replace it with something else. When they strengthen their spirits and make them strong in the Lord, they have no trouble overcoming the temptations. As you will see, those people you meet that are truly free of drugs and alcohol are full of the Word of god and Holy Spirit. They have renewed their minds---old things are passed away, all things are new.

Authors Note:

This book is not written for people who have addictions only - but the same prayers and principles I've found apply to people who have been wounded in spirit, abused as children or adults or are just trying to get their walk with Jesus going. This book is used in my Breakthrough seminars with great success and you will see by reading the testimonies in the back of this book. God is no respecter of persons. What He has done for them, He will do for **you**.

Editors Note: This Book has been the study and outline for healing and deliverance since it was originally published. Miracles and healing manifest from the scriptural principals that bring life and health.

18 REASONS FOR UNANSWERED PRAYERS

Proverbs 28:9 says: "If one turns away his ear from hearing the law, even his prayer is an abomination."

1.   Refusing to hear the truth (Prov. 28:9)
2.   Refusing to humble self (2 Chron. 7:14)
3.   Forsaking God (2 Chron. 15:2)
4.   Provoking God (Dt. 3:26)
5.   Hard heartedness (Zech. 7:12-13)
6.   Lack of charity (Prov. 21:13)
7.   Regarding iniquity (immorality) in heart (Ps. 66:18)
8.   Wrong motives (James 4:3)
9.   Dishonor of companion (I Peter 3:7)
10.   Unbelief (Matt. 17:20-21; 21:22)
11.   Sin (James 4:1-5; Jn. 9:31; Isa. 59:2)
12.   Parading prayer life (Matt. 6:5)
13.   Vain repetitions (Matt. 6:7)
14.   Unforgiveness (Matt. 6:14-15; Mark 11:25,26)
15.   Hypocrisy (Luke 18:9-14)
16.   Being discouraged (Luke 18:1-8)
17.   Worry and anxiety (Phil. 4:6)
18.   Doubting - double mindedness (James 1:5-8)

The reason Christian prayers are not answered is **unbelief**. No man can ask amiss if he is in Christ and asks according to the promises (Jn. 15:7; Mark 11:22-24; Heb. 11:6; James 1:5-8).

TO HAVE THE ABUNDANT LIFE YOU MUST HAVE:

1.   Bible knowledge of who our real enemy is - The devil and demon forces.

2.   Bible knowledge to know that Satan and demonic forces have been totally defeated by Jesus .
(Col. 2:14by canceling the record of debt that stood against us with its legal demands. This he set aside, nailing it to the cross.
I John 3:8 Whoever makes a practice of sinning is of the devil, for the devil has been sinning from the beginning. The reason the Son of God appeared was to destroy the works of the devil.)

3.   Bible knowledge of our authority to drive/cast out demons and Satan from our Canaan Land - YOU MUST DO IT! (Luke 10:19 Heal the sick in it and say to them, 'The kingdom of God has come near to you.'; James 4:7Submit yourselves therefore to God. Resist the devil, and he will flee from you; Mark 16:15 and he said to them, "Go into all the world and proclaim the gospel to the whole creation.)

4.   Bible knowledge of who we are and what we have in Christ. (Ephesians 2: [4] But God, being rich in mercy, because of the great love with which he loved us, [5] even when we were dead in our trespasses, made us alive together with Christ-by grace you have been saved- [6] and raised us up with him and seated us with him in the heavenly places in Christ Jesus, [7] so that in the coming ages he might show the immeasurable riches of his grace in kindness toward us in Christ Jesus. [8] For by grace you have been saved through faith. And this is not your own doing; it is the gift of God, [9] not a result of works, so that no one may boast. [10] For we are his workmanship, created in Christ Jesus for good works, which God prepared beforehand, that we should walk in them.)

STEPS TO MINISTERING HOUSCLEANING

Step I. - Prepare to Receive Ministry from the Holy Spirit*
* DO THIS FIRST

A. You need to go before the Lord and **cleanse yourself**. 1 John 1:9 If we confess our sins, he is faithful and just to forgive us our sins and to cleanse us from all unrighteousness and **submit yourself to God** in prayer.

B. Bind up Satan, i.e. "In the name of Jesus, who has given me authority to use His name, I bind Satan and the principalities and powers of darkness. I bind and cast down spiritual wickedness in heavenly places and render them harmless and ineffective against me and anyone I minister to today. I break the power of all assignments against us, making them null and void. I take authority over all spirits and render them deaf, dumb, blind and unable to manifest in any form or manipulate the person they are in. I paralyze them, forbidding them to speak or tear the person; neither will they transfer onto me or anyone else. I command them to go directly to dark dry places and stay there in the name of Jesus. I command them to come out quietly in the form of yawns or breathing out."

C. "I now ask you, Holy Spirit, to whom I am submitted, to take over as counselor, healer and deliverer, laying aside my flesh and any preconceived ideas, in Jesus name."

NOTE: *Always* do steps A & B before praying any prayers in this book, especially if praying for others.

STEP II. - Forgiveness and Bitter Roots

Take a piece of paper (Worksheet A in the Appendix) and list names of people who have hurt you and people you have hurt. Read Mark 11:25-26 and the Lord's Prayer, Matthew 6:9-13. Forgiveness is a command from the Lord, and if we don't do it, we are the ones who suffer. Unforgiveness opens the door to sickness, and Satan keeps us from Fellowship with the Lord.

Think of a family of four at the dinner table. The son sasses his mother, and the father sends him to his room to think things over. He can come back only if he is sorry and will ask forgiveness. He is still a member of the family, but is not getting his benefits. He can stay in his room and sulk, lick his wounds and be hungry all night---OR he can think it over, go back and apologize to his mother, and at least get in on the dessert. As soon as he says "Sorry," in true repentance, his benefits are restored and as soon as we pray and release people from the bondage we've held them in, we are released and forgiven by the Lord and our benefits are restored. Many times people receive healing (physical as well as emotional) the moment they do this.

It is important to know that forgiveness does not mean the other person is right, but if you desire to do things God's way, He will handle the people who have wronged you. This helps if you are holding on to one particular person and incident.

Salvation is not a magic wand. It is a fallacy to think, "Everything will be OK from now on. I'll just float through life with Jesus out there ahead of me, straightening all the curves, whipping all my enemies." "No more problems for me!" Being a Christian is a new, wonderful experience, BUT we still have to deal with our flesh and past hurts that have accumulated over the years, even some spirits that have made themselves at home with us! It's true, we've been forgiven all our past sins, but many of us have not forgiven those who hurt us along the way; we have not forgiven ourselves, not to mention the case we have against God! Lots of frustration has turned into anger and formed bitter roots in us that have to go.

You need to release people from your judgment to God's judgment. Bitter roots are like dandelions --- you mow them off today, but they are back in two days because the roots are still in the ground. Those roots have to be destroyed, pulled out, or the law of sowing and reaping will continue. It's the same with us. We really can't have a meaningful, loving walk with Jesus until we get cleaned up---sozo'd(the Greek word "sozo" means saved from hell, healed of all diseases and delivered from the power of Satan)---set free, and many of us are holding ourselves prisoner through unforgiveness. Mark 11:25-26: "And whenever you stand praying, forgive, if you have anything against anyone, so that your Father also who is in heaven may forgive you your trespasses."

Forgiveness is the key that unlocks the door to wholeness. It is a commandment. If we want God's Word to work in our lives, it is really for our sake, not others'. If we don't forgive, unforgiveness will:

> 1. Rot our bones.
> 2. Open the door to sickness.
> 3. Keep us from fellowship with the Father.

Remember:

Forgiveness does not mean the other person is right---nor is it a feeling. It can be defined as giving up our right to hurt someone because they've hurt us! Where there is strife, there is every evil work!

You need to pray the Lord's Prayer daily and forgive those who trespass against you, so you may walk in right standing with God.

Scriptures on forgiveness:

Matthew 6:9   Lord's Prayer

Matthew 18:21 Peter---How many times do I forgive my brother?

Matthew 18:15 If your brother sins against you---take to church if necessary.

Mark 11:25-26 Stand praying, forgive, so Father can forgive you.

Matthew 5:43-44 Love enemies---pray for those who curse you. Do to others as you would have them do to you.

Luke 16:11   Son who spent his inheritance---father ran to meet him and forgive him.

I John 2:9   Anyone who hates his brother is in darkness.

I John 1:9   If we confess our sins, God is faithful and just to forgive us and cleanse us from all unrighteousness.

Read Psalm 32 It talks about how great we feel when we've been forgiven and how terrible we felt before we finally gave in.

Bitter Root Judgment

Hebrews 12:15: "See to it that no one fails to obtain the grace of God; that "no root of bitterness" springs up and causes trouble, and by it many become defiled."

Matthew 7:12 "So whatever you wish that others would do to you, do also to them, for this sums up the Law and the prophets."

Galatians 6:7: "Do not be deceived: God is not mocked, for whatever one sows, that he will also reap."

Bitterness comes in stages!

1. Hurt
2. Disappointment
3. Resentment
4. Anger
5. Hate
6. Revenge---by this stage a root has formed.

Some bitter root judgments will cause us to judge people for how they act and appear and then expect others or ourselves never to be that way, like my judgment of my father and mother. We're so surprised to find out we are just like them!

There is another type of bitter root judgment that puts an expectancy of fear on us and those we come into contact with in the future. We fear we will be like that. When a person can never seem to please one parent or another (we are to honor our parents, remember?), the bitter root judgment turns into the expectancy that the future man or woman in our lives will be the same as the parent we are judging. We fear that we will never be accepted or able to please our mate in the same way!

16

Author John Sanford tells about a young man who judged his mother, who had grown fat and sloppy. She kept a dirty house, which repulsed him, so he judged her. His wife, before marriage, never could please her father, and she judged him. All went well after they were married, until the wife got pregnant. After the baby came, she didn't lose her excess weight. Her husband became critical and upset (like her father) and she, because of frustration, began to eat and eat and became very insecure! She couldn't keep the house neat and their judgments and reactions spun to more and more painful levels until she was living with any angry demon and he was living with a food addict.

They were caught in a trap and found themselves powerless to stop.

The Law of Judgment that says "the measure we mete out and receive" had gone into effect. Even when our judgments are true about a parent, the law of Deut. 5:16 about honoring parents goes into effect and ensures that in whatever regard we are harshly judging our parents, life will not go well for us. Our judgment was a seed sown which by law must someday be repaid!

Galatians 6:7: "Do not be deceived: God is not mocked, for whatever one sows, that will he also reap."
Sowing and reaping can be devastating: when you plant one seed you get back many. Did you ever notice how many seeds are in a cantaloupe? A small seed of resentment, anger or sweet revenge held against a family member even from childhood, may be sown and forgotten, but the longer it remains undetected or neglected, the larger it grows. So a mustard seed can become a huge, tall tree if we don't wake up.

The Good News is that the full legal demand of the law of sowing and reaping was fulfilled in the pain of the cross, upon the body of our Lord Jesus. We still have our part to do; the cross is not automatic. We must **confess** and **repent**, otherwise we reap in full, despite the mercy of the cross.

The man who judged his mother for obesity was due to reap obesity. Who more likely than his wife? His judgment drew him to a woman who was likely to have a weight problem, then it pushed his wife to gain weight! His seed was returning like a mighty wind. His wife, under its powerful thrust, was bound to fulfill it. She had her own set of judgments going against her, and her seed sown was reaped through him.

Here are the laws we all, single or married, face:

1.Life will go well for us in every area in which we can honor our parents, and will not go well with us in the areas we cannot honor them.

2.We will receive harm in the same areas of life in which we have meted judgment against others.

3.We will most assuredly reap what we have sown. These laws for the healing of relationships are the most powerful keys God has revealed to His people. Just consider what each of us is bringing into a relationship from our past attitudes and behavior.

Examine some facts:

*People raised in alcoholic, drug-related families, either end up marrying an alcoholic or become one themselves.

*People with domineering mothers attract the same.

So if we've judged, even as a child, it has to be dealt with; otherwise it can further defile us. Hebrews 12:15 says, "See to it that *no root of bitterness* springs up (means suddenly showing itself to surface) and causes trouble." Hate and resentment have the deepest of roots.

Read this prayer out loud:

Dear Heavenly Father, I come to you in Jesus' Name, asking you to forgive me for holding grudges. I am sorry for the way I have acted and I rededicate my life to you today, Lord Jesus.

I ask you to come into my heart afresh today. Please forgive me for not living for you as I should have. I receive you afresh as my Savior, Healer and Deliverer. I crown you King and Lord over every part of my life. I will live for You to the best of my ability from now on. Thank You for Your love and mercy.

I renounce Satan and his demons; they no longer have a hold on me. I am under the blood of Jesus---HE IS MY LORD.

Today I choose to release the people on this list, not because I "feel" forgiveness or because they are right, but because I choose to be obedient to you, Father. I realize your ways are higher than my ways, and today I release them from my hurt, my disappointment, my resentment, my anger, my hate, my unforgiveness and my bitterness, especially my parents and family, or anyone that I have made bitter-root judgments against. I release them from my judgment and plow up the ground where the bad seeds were sown, turn under those bitter roots, and plant new seeds of love, acceptance and forgiveness.

I thank You that I can bind Satan and break the hold he had on me in regard to this matter and break his power over my life. I make null and void all things I've reaped from the past. As I bind him according to Matthew 18:18, I know what I bind on earth is bound in heaven, and I command him to leave, in the Mighty Name of Jesus! Do not return. And now I loose the spirit of agape love and the compassion of Jesus as Spirit of Truth in my life to set me FREE!!!

Thank You, Lord, I will no longer reap from those bitter roots that I sowed. Please have those I have hurt release me also, Lord. However, if you have anyone you specifically want me to contact, I will do it. Just bring them to my heart when I leave here today and I will either call, write or go see them.

Tear up the paper and put it in the wastebasket. Cup your hands in front of you and say to the Lord:

Lord Jesus, here are the people I have hurt and the ones who have hurt me. I release them to you. I pray for those who have despitefully used me. I pray for my enemies as you have commanded and ask You to bless them and save them in Your precious Name. You say to cast my cares upon You because You care for me. Thank You, Lord. These people are no longer my problem; they are Yours! (Throw up hands to God and let them go!) Thank You, Lord for setting me free. Please heal me of my hurts in regard to these people. Please change my heart about them as only you can do!

Father God, I now release You of the things I have held against You. I've been wrong and I'm sorry. I know you are a loving, caring Father, and I am grateful for Your forgiveness. Because You have forgiven and released me. I can and do forgive myself! Hallelujah!

You may have some tears. They are tears of relief. You'll see for yourself that unforgiveness takes its toll on a person's physical body, as well as emotions. You might read books such as "There is Power in Forgiveness", by Marilyn Hickey, or "Telling Yourself the Truth", by William Backus and Marie Chapian.

You will now take the paper (Worksheet B in the Appendix) for inner healing of the wounds you just forgave people for. Please prayerfully fill in the following:

1 - Age incident happened, i.e. 5 years old.

2 - Feeling when it occurred, i.e., fear: couldn't sleep for weeks.

3 - Brief note on what happened, i.e., watched horror movie with brothers and sisters.

Remember, the people who caused the hurts are in the hands of the Lord; it is time to face the problems they caused and get them healed. Otherwise, they are still festering and will eventually open doors for these feelings to return.

Repeat Step 1 (Preparation for Ministry) before EACH prayer if you are ministering to someone else and time has elapsed between prayers, or you are going through this workbook a prayer or two at a time. You must bind the enemy before you start again.

STEP III. Spiritual Housecleaning

Before you can begin your spiritual housecleaning, you need to know something about the spirits you are going to evict. There are:

(1) The Good Spirit - Holy Spirit of God

(2) Evil Spirits (strongmen) - from Satan

When ministering at "Hotel", [1]God's Holy Spirit would show me the strongholds Satan would get over people to hold them in bondage to their sickness. There are many strongmen listed in the Bible, such as:

* Spirit of fear - most common
* Spirit of jealousy (anger, hate, bitterness, etc.)
* Lying spirit
* Spirits of divination and familiar spirit
* Perverse and unclean spirits...perverted sex,

homosexuality, etc.
* Spirit of haughtiness (pride) unforgiveness
* Spirit of heaviness
* Spirit of infirmity
* Dumb and deaf spirit
* Spirit of bondage, drugs and alcohol
* Seducing spirit
* Spirit of error
* Spirit of anti-Christ
* Spirit of death and self-destruction

[1]Evelyn Diment, God's Get-Well Hotel, U.S. Graphics, Tulsa, 1987. The telling of the miraculous ministry of healing the Lord gave her.

Most common are spirits of fear, jealousy, haughtiness (pride) and bondage.

We are constantly being exposed to all kinds of spirits -- spirits that come as "angels of light" yet are disruptive and destructive. These spirits are transferable from one to another, but only if a person is open or unprotected. Let no believer who loves God, who is walking in the Spirit and not in sin, fear transference or demon possession! *1 Cor. 2:11-14:* "For who knows a person's thoughts except the spirit of that person, which is in him? So also no one comprehends the thoughts of God except the Spirit of God. Now we have received not the spirit of the world, but the Spirit who is from God, that we might understand the things freely given us by God. And we impart this in words not taught by human wisdom but taught by the Spirit, interpreting spiritual truths to those who are spiritual. The natural person does not accept the things of the Spirit of God, for they are folly to him, and he is not able to understand them because they are spiritually discerned.S

Since the natural man does not understand the things of God, it follows that the natural man will also not understand the things of Satan; however, if the spiritual man understands the things of the Spirit of God, he should also understand the things of the spirit of the devil. But, here is where the problem is: while many of us are instructed on the things of the Holy Spirit, few have had instruction on the things of the unholy spirit!

Some Christians make light of this and say, "I give all my time and thought to the Lord. I have no time or interest in the workings of Satan". Sounds good and honorable and spiritual, doesn't it? But unfortunately, it is unrealistic. Even some ministers are this way because they do not understand the seriousness of the subject and the craftiness and intent of the enemy.

After you become clean new creatures in Christ, you will be instructed on how to stay clean and safe, because God equips us for every problem if we'll seriously apply ourselves to His instructions! Unless we have the Spirit of God dwelling in us, we will not grasp this subject. Even born-again, Spirit-filled children of God should prayerfully ask the Holy Spirit for openness and understanding. The enemy will do everything possible to keep this truth from us, because it is the weapon he is using to bring disarray, confusion and destruction to the children of God. He is doing just that through the weapon of transference of spirits. He has repeatedly brought division and confusion by using strong personal ties among the disorganized. He has used the spirit of rebellion to bring splits, splinter groups, cults and doctrines, and disarray to God's people. Strong-willed people have imposed their spirit upon the submissive and led them captive to spiritual slaughter. But, glory to God, we have weapons. As God's servants we have a remedy, and now we have a God-given right to "bind and loose" in the spirit world.

Matthew 18:18: "Truly, I say to you, whatever you bind on earth shall be bound in heaven, and whatever you loose on earth shall be loosed in heaven."

You know as a believer that the Spirit of the Lord can come upon you as a direct and sovereign act of God. There's also the "evil spirit" that can come upon a person--- a direct and sovereign act of Satan--- but remember, this cannot happen to believers who abide under the covering of the Blood of Christ! We can still be attacked; this is where we use our weapons.

The Word says the natural man will not understand, because he depends on his five senses.

During "Hotel" days God began teaching me through His Word:

1. How to help people receive their healings and why some were having difficulty in doing that. He said, "My people perish for lack of knowledge", (Knowledge about "sozo", Greek for saved, healed and delivered). Isaiah 53 tells how Jesus went to the whipping post and received stripes, so we could be healed and set free. Lack of knowledge about that keeps many from getting healed.

Mark 16:15-20 tells us that we believers will have signs following us. We will be setting people free, healing the sick and watching them recover, which is a process. God wants us healed and set free, and He doesn't care what method we use--- Him, doctors, medicine--- as long as we recognize Him in all of it. Many doctors say they only stop symptoms so that God can do the healing. Our bodies are made to heal themselves. In John 14:12 Jesus said, "....whoever believes in me will also do the works I do; and greater works than these will he do, because I am going to the Father".

2. Our lack of knowledge about our enemy who, 'as a roaring lion, walking about, seeking whom he may devour" (1 Peter 5:8). Jesus said, "He (Satan) is a liar and the father of lies", a deceiver. If he can deceive us into thinking God is punishing us with sickness or being crippled or addicted, he'll get the upper hand. Remember, there was no sickness until the fall!

3. Our lack of knowledge about why Jesus came to this earth. He is GOD in the flesh. In Luke 4:18-19, Jesus states that "The Spirit of the Lord is upon me..."

a) To preach the gospel to the poor.
b) To heal the brokenhearted.
c) To preach deliverance to the captives.
d) To give recovery of sight to the blind.
e) To set at liberty those who are bruised. Acts 10:38:"...God anointed Jesus of Nazareth with the Holy Spirit and with power. He went about doing good and healing all that were oppressed of the devil; for God was with Him.

4. Many have lack of knowledge that Jesus was victorious over the devil and took the keys of death and hell away from him making a show of him openly. AND because of that He transferred that power and authority to us through the Holy Spirit - and expected us to continue in His footsteps till He comes back.

Luke 10:19: "Behold, I give you authority to tread on serpents and scorpions, and over all the power of the enemy, and nothing shall by any means hurt you".

James 4:7: "Submit yourselves to God. Resist the devil and he will flee from you".

1 John 5:18 tells us that when we are doing our best to please God, the evil one touches us not!!!

In 2 Timothy 2:26: "...and they may come to their senses and escape from the snare of the devil, after being captured by him to do his will."

5. We've had lack of knowledge about the conditions we must meet in order to have God's promise work in our lives, i.e., to walk in holiness, forgiveness and love.

6. A great many have lack of knowledge about forgiveness *(Mark 11:25-26)*. We hold not only ourselves in bondage, but others by our unforgiveness in anger, licking our wounds and contemplating sweet revenge.

7. We've had lack of knowledge about spiritual warfare. How do we clean these out of our houses?

In Matthew 18:18: Jesus teaches that "...Whatever you bind on earth shall be bound in heaven, and whatever you loose on earth shall be loosed in heaven."

Luke 11:17-26: "Jesus...said to them: 'Every kingdom divided against itself is laid waste, and a divided household falls. And if Satan also is divided against himself, how will his kingdom stand? For you say that I cast out demons by Beelzebub. And if I drive out demons by Beelzebub, by whom do your sons drive them out? Therefore they will be your judges. But if it is by the finger of God that I cast out demons, then the kingdom of God has come upon you. When a strong man, fully armed, guards his own place, his goods are safe; but when one stronger than he attacks him and overcomes him, he takes away his armor in which he trusted and divides his spoils.

Whoever is not with me is against me, and he who does not gather with me, scatters. When an unclean spirit comes out of a person, it passes through waterless places seeking rest, and finding none it says, 'I will return to my house from which I came.' And when it comes, it finds the house swept and put in order. Then it goes and brings seven other spirits more evil than itself, and they enter and dwell there. And the last state of that person is worse than the first."

So we put on our armor (Eph. 6:10-20) and then bind (Matt: 18:18) the strongman. Curse him and destroy the fruit (sickness or spirit) and order him out; bind and loose; forbid him to return; and fill the vacancy with the power of God and proper spirits, i.e., replace a lying spirit with the spirit of truth; and repair damage done by strongman; take back the territory he spoiled and call things back into order-- God's order.

Remember the parable of the sower (Luke 8:1-15). It says the enemy will come back to steal healing or new freedom, but now you have knowledge. You resist him, bind him up, forbid him to return. And use the powerful name of Jesus to send him on the run.

How to keep free? Renew our minds-- become transformed by the Word of God. A good defense is a good offense. Start out each day by putting on armor, getting under the Blood, and telling the devil where to go. Get under the prayer of protection! Plan to do this daily from now on.

I Peter 5:8: "Be sober minded; be watchful. Your adversary the devil prowls around like a roaring lion, seeking someone to devour." We will do greater works! (John 14:12) So it is up to us to stop him, and God has given us all the tools we need. Everything that bothers us is not the devil, but we must be able to tell whether it is our flesh we are resisting or the adversary. Then either way we know how to pray and take a stand.

Today you will receive housecleaning of spirits that have made their homes in you. This indwelling happens as we go along in life before we serve the Lord. A trauma comes and a spirit of fear (as an example) enters us, opening the door for others, such as lying spirits, jealous spirits, angry spirits, haughty spirits of pride, etc., to come in and form a personality in us. When these spirits are made to leave, we actually become the person God intended us to be and great changes take place in our personalities. We really feel born again, clean and free!! No person would have all these spirits in them. We do it this way in order not to miss one or let Satan play tricks on us; like throwing out the net for the catch-- keeping the good fish and tossing out the bad.

Prayer for Spiritual Housecleaning (Deliverance from Spirits)

Pray this prayer out loud:

Dear Heavenly Father, I come to you in Jesus' name, recognizing you as my Lord, Savior, Healer and Deliverer. You know all my problems-- all the things that bind, torment, defile and harass me. Today I refuse to accept anything more from Satan, and I loose myself from every dark spirit, from every evil influence, from every satanic bondage, and from every spirit in me that is not the Spirit of God. I bind all these spirits up according to Matthew 18:18 where it says that whatever I bind on earth is bound in heaven, and whatever I loose on earth is loosed in heaven.

I ask you, Father, to forgive me for allowing these spirits to manifest in my life and to use my body for their home. I purpose in my heart to serve you from now on.

Satan, I rebuke you and all your evil spirits. I renounce any occult activities I've been involved in and renounce these strongmen and curse their fruit in me as Jesus did the fig tree. Right now I bind up and command these strongmen and their fruit to go directly to dark, dry places and stay there in Jesus' Name. Jesus has given me authority to use His Name, which is above all names. I now command;

* The spirit of divination
* Familiar spirits
* Spirit of jealousy, anger and unforgiveness
* Lying spirit, guilt, self-condemnation
* Perverse and unclean spirits - pornography and lust, fornication, homosexuality and adultery
* Spirit of haughtiness (pride)
* Spirit of heaviness, depression and oppression
* Spirit of whoredoms (gluttony)
* Spirit of infirmity, sickness and disease

Dumb and deaf spirit
Spirit of bondage (especially addiction to drugs, alcohol, cigarettes and entertainment)
Spirit of witchcraft and rebellion
Spirit of lethargy
Controlling spirits, judgmental critical spirits
Spirit of fear, anxiety, tormenting driving spirits
Seducing spirits
Spirit of antichrist
Spirit of error
Spirit of confusion
Spirit of death (self-destruction)
and all their fruit to GO. "

Take a deep breath and say *"go...GO...**GO**!"* The spirits have to leave, and the rest will leave through the openings in your body, such as your pores, and yawns. Now pray and Jesus will fill you with the right spirits, so there will be no empty places in you and no need to fear their coming back and bringing more friends, for these are going to dark, dry places and cannot return.

It is up to you now to apply what you will learn, to walk free and not let Satan con you into letting new spirits come in. You will learn how to walk free and stay that way. After today, if you've had a drug or alcohol problem, you will never desire another drink or fix---your body will not go into withdrawal, because you will call it back into chemical balance. It will be as if you have never drank or used in your whole life. As you call the good spirits into you, it is the fulfilling of the scripture, "...The old has passed away; behold, the new has come". (*2Corinthians 5:17*) You are in essence now a new creature in Christ Jesus. Speak to the Father now in confidence:

In Jesus' Name, I now call these spirits to come in and fill me to overflowing with God and His love. I loose upon myself the Holy Spirit and all His gifts:
The Love of God
The spirit of Truth to set me free
Power, love and a sound mind
A good and excellent spirit
The spirit of purity
A humble and contrite spirit

27

* The spirit of holiness
* The joy of the Lord
* The garment of praise
* The oil of gladness
* The comforter
* The gifts of healing and miracles, for by His stripes I
  am healed
* The spirit of adoption
* The spirit of life, for no weapon formed against me
  will prosper

What I have loosed on earth is loosed in heaven, and I call my body into chemical balance. Thank you, Lord. There will be no withdrawals or D.T.'s; it will be as if I never drank or used. I speak to my thyroid and command it to function properly. I speak wholeness to my metabolism and my hormone balance. I command my immune system to function properly and my white cells to rise up and defeat and sickness in my mind and body today.

In the name of Jesus I command the pituitary gland to restructure the signals to my body, and for all the organs, glands, bones and tissues to respond and be restored to the perfect order of God. I thank You, Father, for Your special touch now upon me (or this brother or sister, if you are ministering to someone else) *this very moment. In Jesus' Name.*

Now repeat this prayer out loud:

Thank You, Father, for setting me free. I confess that my body is a temple for the Holy Spirit; I am redeemed, cleansed, sanctified, justified, healed and delivered by the blood of Jesus. Therefore, Satan, from this day forward you have no place in me and no power over me, through the blood of Jesus.

Rejoice; it's done. You may feel a little light headed or a little dizzy or greatly relieved. However, some say they do not feel any different, or that they feel like going right out and having a drink. These people need more ministry, letting them know we do not go by feelings, but by the truth of the Word of God; that in James 4:7 it says to submit to God and tell the devil to flee and he has to go, no matter how we feel. In the case of James Robinson, it took two days for him to feel the claw was gone from his mind, so do not be discouraged, but believe.

It's important that you're honest with yourself about how badly you really want to be free. Now is the time to take a stand against Satan, knowing the Lord *will* see you through. I it to understand double-mindedness, as explained in James 1:2-8: "Count it all joy, my brothers, when you meet trials of various kinds, for you know that the testing of your faith produces steadfastness. And let steadfastness have its full effect, that you may be perfect and complete lacking in nothing. If any of you lack wisdom, let him ask God, who gives generously to all without reproach, and it will be given him. But let him ask in faith, with no doubting, for the one who doubts is like a wave of the sea that is driven and tossed by the wind. For that person must not suppose that he will receive anything from the Lord; he is a double minded man, unstable in all his ways."

Once we have done all we know to do, stand in faith because whom the Son sets free is free indeed! It is rare that anyone will go through these prayers and feel nothing--- it is usually a sign that your mind was not made up to give everything over to Jesus--- but it has happened, and you need to know the cause of it. It is a sign that the principles of the parable sower have gone into effect. Mark 4:13-25: "And he said to them, "Do you not understand this parable? How then will you understand all the parables? The sower sows the word. And these are the ones along the path, where the word is sown: when they hear, Satan immediately comes and takes away the word that is sown in them. And these are the ones sown on rocky ground: the ones who, when they hear the word, immediately receive it with joy. And they have no root in themselves, but endure for a while; then, when tribulation or persecution arises on the account of the word, they immediately they fall away. And others are the ones sown among the thorns. They are those that hear the word, but the cares of the world and the deceitfulness of riches and desires for other things enter in and choke the word, and it proves unfruitful. But those that were sown on the good soil are the ones that hear the word accept it and bear fruit, thirtyfold and sixtyfold and a hundredfold". And he said to them, "Is a lamp brought in to be put under a basket, or under a bed, and not on a stand? For nothing is hidden except to be made manifest; nor is anything secret except to come to light. If anyone has ears to hear, let him hear". And he said to them, "Pay attention to what you hear: with the measure you use, it will be measured to you and still more will be added to you. For to the one who has more will be given, and from the one who has not, even what he has will be taken away."

The enemy will not give you up that easily, but now that he is on the outside and Jesus is on the inside, the battle is fixed. It's a cinch. You just need to set your mind to doing it Jesus' way.

Luke 8:12--- It's a fact the enemy will come immediately to steal the Word (of healing, deliverance and salvation) out of our hearts the minute we have been prayed for, but he is a loser and we need to help people not lose heart, but rise up and fight for what is ours.

Daily do intercession and warfare saying the "Armor of God" and "Prayer of Protection" twice a day out loud. This is a must do plan till Jesus comes!

Armor of God: Ephesians 6:10-20

I am strong in you, Lord, and in the power of Your might. I put on the whole armor of God and do stand against the plans of the devil. In the name of Jesus, I bind Satan and the principalities, the powers, the rulers of the darkness of this world. I bind and cast down spiritual wickedness in high places and render them harmless and ineffective against me and my loved ones. I resist you, devil, in the name of Jesus, I stand my ground.

I have the belt of truth buckled around my waist--- the truth of God that sets me free! I have on the breastplate of righteousness that covers my body, my heart and vital organs and shows I am in right standing with my God! My feet are shod with the preparation of the gospel of peace, and I take those feet and tread on serpents and scorpions, for I have been given authority of all of your power. I have on the helmet of salvation that covers my head securely, for I have the mind of Christ. The only spirit I will follow is the Spirit of the living God that lives inside me and speaks to me from within.

I take the shield of faith and quench every fiery dart you throw at me, devil! I take the sword of the Spirit which is the Word of God, and pierce through your wicked plans, for it is written all I have to do is submit myself to God, and tell you to flee, and you have to go... so GO! in the name of Jesus.

I place the blood of Jesus over me, my family, my home, my ministry, my place of employment, places where we stay when we travel, modes of transportation on land sea or air, my bank accounts, my debts, my car and possessions --- all of which belong to you God--- and I serve notice that your power is broken, devil, over me and mine, in Jesus' Name. Thank you, Father. Send my people my way to minister to today. Amen

A Prayer of Protection

Father, because I dwell in the secret place of the most high, I pray that I will remain stable and fixed under the shadow of You, Almighty God, whose power no one can withstand. I say of You, Lord, "You are my refuge and my fortress, my God on whom I rely and confidently trust." For You deliver me from the snare of the fowler deadly pestilence terrors of the night, evil plots of the wicked, and destruction or sudden death. Wherever I am, I am safe from fire, earthquakes, freak weather storms, power outages, gas leaks, thieves, or evil people with murder rape or violence on their minds. Safe from volcano eruptions, high winds of every kind – acts of war, acts of God even being trapped or buried alive in anything that exists on this earth, the earth itself, the waters thereof or anything that flies in air! A thousand will fall at my side, ten thousand at my right hand – but it won't come near me – only with my eyes shall I see the reward of the wicked --- and because I have made you my refuge, no evil shall befall me, nor shall any plague or calamity come near my dwelling that will cripple, maim, blind or kill me because you have already delivered me from destruction, sickness and accidents. And whether I take a walk, ride a bicycle, motorcycle, van, truck, bus – in a car, train, plane, or boat, or swim, ski, skate, of fly, I am safe. For your angles have been given charge over me to accompany (and defend) me in all ways, lest I even dash my foot against a stone.

Thank You that You will never leave or forsake me, but as I call upon You, You will be with me even in times of trouble to deliver me, satisfying me with a long and healthy life! All this is true because I have set my love on You, and I know Your Name, I have made You this family's habitation. Be it done unto me and my family according to your Word! Amen.

Step IV. Generational Curses

Exodus 20:4-6 "You shall not make for yourself a carved image, or any likeness of anything that is in heaven above, or that is in the earth beneath, or that is in the water under the earth. You shall not bow down to them or serve them, for I the LORD your God am a jealous God, visiting the iniquity of the fathers on the children to the third and the fourth generation of those who hate me, but showing steadfast love to thousands of those who love me and keep my commandments.

Things are passed down through generations to us through the bloodlines of our ancestors; things like diabetes, heart disease, ect. There are familiar spirits, alcoholism and addictions included, that may follow families. Not knowing who is in our ancestral background may have been involved in witchcraft or occult practices, we take no chances.
We pray:

In the name of Jesus Christ, I now renounce, break and loose myself from all generation curses, psychic heredity, demonic holds, psychic powers, bondages-addictions to drug and alcohol- bonds of physical or mental illnesses, or curses upon me or my family line as a result of sin, transgressions, evil behavior, occult or psychic involvements of myself, my parents, or any of my ancestors

I break the power of all evil words spoken out against me from the day I was conceived in my mother's womb until this moment, in Jesus' Name.

Thank you Lord Jesus, for setting us free!

Step V. Soul Ties

Can a man carry fire next to his chest, and his clothes not be burned? Or can one walk on hot coals, and his feet not be scorched? So he that goes to his neighbor's wife; none who touches her will go unpunished... He who commits adultery lacks sense; he who does it destroys himself. (Proverbs 6:27,32)

In his book Seductions Exposed,[2]Gary Greenwald, Eagles Nest Publications, Santa Ana, 1988.

"Just as our soul ties to the Lord make us one with Him, when two people become bonded together in marriage, they also become one. Their soul ties are so powerful that they may in time walk, talk, and act alike. When one starts a sentence, the other may finish it."

"They may even begin to look alike. In love they absorb the best from each other; in strife they absorb the worst from each other. Because these soul ties are so strong, the marriage covenant was made to never be broken. <u>Divorce is particularly devastating because two intertwined souls have to be literally ripped and torn apart.</u> The intermingling cords of each other's souls cannot be separated without inflicting deep wounds upon one another."

"If you listen to covenant marriage vows, you will witness two people becoming soul tied through confession. However, the marriage bed is the final consummation of two people becoming one flesh and one soul. The soul tie formed through sexual union of marriage is unique – man was created to have this bond with only **one** person!"

"God has made the sexual union to be whole being to whole being... spirit to spirit, soul to soul, body to body. This union is the reason marriage is such a wonderful covenant. In the beginning when God created man in the Garden of Eden, he took a part of the man to make the woman. The original language says that He actually made them and called them Adam. Their unity was so perfect that they had the same name. It was only after they sinned and a separation came between them and God, that woman was called Eve and the man was called Adam."

"Since the sexual union of marriage ties two souls as one, what do you think happens if a person commits fornication or adultery with another person outside of this marriage? Actually, his soul becomes mysteriously knit and tied to the other person also--- they cleave together just as in marriage. The soul ties formed through illicit sexual involvement can be just as strong and binding as those formed through the marriage covenant."

"Sexual involvement can form such entangling tentacles of soul ties that it is extremely difficult to break off the relationship. Have you ever heard the expression, 'I've got you under my skin?' As a teenager I worked at a dairy with Chad, a pastor's son. Chad was promiscuous and often bragged about his sexual conquests. However one of Chad's girlfriends was a sweet, moral girl who refused to go to bed with him. Frustrated over her reluctance, one day he over powered her and raped her. After that experience she mysteriously became enslaved to him and constantly called him wanting to be with him--- he was 'under her skin' through a soul tie. Sadly, he quickly grew tired of her and discarded her. She was no longer a challenge.

She needed help from people outside her environment in order to be set free. To indicate how strong these soul ties are, Genesis tells us that the desire of the woman shall be for her husband or for the man who becomes her first soul tied partner (Her first sexual partner). *Genesis 3:16 says '... your desire shall be for your husband, and he shall rule over you...'*

"God designed the universe to function with natural and spiritual laws that bring freedom when obeyed, but bondage and destruction when broken and violated. Just as two souls can be knit or made to cleave together in a covenant relationship, they can also be tied or knit together to form bondage and enslavement. Sexual union was ordained by God to make two marriage partners one flesh before God, but promiscuous premarital and extramarital affairs can mysteriously tie ones soul to many partners.

"Most individuals have no concept how promiscuity outside of marriage scatters their souls and destroys their ability to commit to one partner. One of the purposes of marriage is to provide for the sexual need of two partners. The bible tells the marriage partners that they are to be a continual fountain through which the other is satisfied... a cistern not to

34

be shared with others. Proverbs 5:15, 17-19 says, *"Drink water from your own cistern, flowing water from your own well… Let them be for yourself alone, and not for strangers with you. Let your fountain be blessed, and rejoice in the wife of your youth, a lovely deer, a graceful doe. Let her breasts fill you at all times with delight; be intoxicated always in her love."*

The tragedy is that few people understand the incredible consequences of the supposedly casual affair. In 1 Corinthians 6:16, 18: Paul challenges *"Or do you not know that he who is joined (sexually) to a prostitute (any sexual partner outside of marriage) becomes one body with her? For, it is written, "Two will become one flesh"… Flee from sexual immorality. Every other sin a person commits is outside the body, but the sexually immoral person sins against his own body.*

"Because he has joined himself body, soul and spirit to another, such a person is soul tied and 'one flesh' with his sexual partner. As we have seen, this will work for either blessing or destruction.

"You may be involved or becoming involved in a sexual relationship right now. You may justify what you are doing by saying 'We are different. We really love each other. We have made a commitment to each other. We plan to marry someday.' But God says it is a sin and it will bring the eventual destruction and not blessings to your life. God never makes exceptions to His laws for you or for anyone else! Romans 11:16 states, *'For if the first fruits (start or beginning) be holy, the lump is also holy; and if the root be holy so are the branches.'*

A relationship begun in righteous and holy actions will often bring forth blessed and holy branches. On the other hand, a relationship begun in sin and fornication will many times bring forth evil branches and fruit. This could include adulterous cheating, divorces, and even children that indulge in immorality.

The Bible says when we join ourselves to a mate, we become one flesh. When we commit adultery, we sin against our own body and bring a curse upon ourselves. We become defiled and if we are married and are having an affair on the side, we bring that defilement to our mate. These must be broken. A man's soul can also be scattered and destroyed through adulterous relationships. (Proverbs 27-29, 32)

There is nothing more destructive than sexual promiscuity. 1 Corinthians 6:18 says, *'Flee from sexual immorality. Every other sin a person commits is outside the body, but the sexually immoral person sins against his own body.'*

Genesis 2:24: *'Therefore a man shall leave his father and his mother, and hold fast to his wife, and they shall be one flesh.'*

Genesis 3:16: *To the woman he said, 'I will surely multiply your pain in childbearing; in pain you shall bring forth children. Your desire shall be for your husband, and he shall rule over you.'*

1 Corinthians 7:2-5*: "But because of the temptation to sexual immorality, each man should have his own wife and each woman her own husband. The husband should give to his wife her conjugal rights, and likewise the wife to her husband. For the wife does not have authority over her own body, but the husband does. Likewise the husband does not have authority over his own body, but the wife does. Do not deprive one another, except perhaps by agreement for a limited time, that you may devote yourselves to prayer; but then come together again, so that Satan may not tempt you because of your lack of self-control.*

2 Timothy 3:1-7: *"But understand this, that in the last days there will come times of difficulty. For people will be lovers of self, lovers of money, proud, arrogant, abusive, disobedient to their parents, ungrateful, unholy, heartless, unappeasable, slanderous, without self-control, brutal, not loving good, treacherous, reckless, swollen with conceit, lovers of pleasure rather than lovers of God, having the appearance of godliness, but denying its power. Avoid such people. For among them are those who creep into households and capture weak women, burdened with sins and led astray by various passions, always learning and never able to arrive at a knowledge of the truth."*

Proverbs 5:15-23: *"Drink water from your own cistern, flowing water from your own well. Should your springs be scattered abroad, streams of water in the streets? Let them be for yourself alone, and not for strangers with you. Let your fountain be blessed, and rejoice in the wife of your youth, a lovely deer, a graceful doe. Let her breasts fill you at all times with delight; be intoxicated always in her love. Why should you be intoxicated, my son, with a forbidden woman and*

embrace the bosom of an adulteress? For a man's ways
are before the eyes of the LORD, *and he ponders all his paths.*
The iniquities of the wicked ensnare him, and he is held fast in
the cords of his sin. He dies for lack of discipline, and because of
his great folly he is led astray.

Pray this prayer:

Father, in the name of Jesus, I submit my soul, my desires
and my emotions to your Spirit. I confess as sin, all my
promiscuous, premarital sexual relationships and all sexual
relationships outside of marriage. I confess all my ungodly spirit,
soul, and body ties as sin. I thank you for forgiving me and
cleansing me right now!

Father, thank You for giving me the keys of your kingdom,
the keys of spiritual authority. What I bind is bound and what I
loose is loosed. In Jesus' Name I ask You to cut and loose me from
all soul ties to past sexual partners and ungodly relationships.
Please uproot the tentacles of sexual bondage, of emotional
longings and dependencies and of enslaving thoughts. I bind,
renounce, and resist and evil spirits that have reinforced those
soul ties or may have been transferred to me or my mate and
have defiled us through evil associations.

Please cleanse my soul and help me forget all illicit unions
so that I am free to give my soul totally to You and to my mate or
future mate. Father, I receive Your forgiveness for all past sexual
sins. Thank You for remembering my sins no more. Thank You
for cleansing me from all unrighteousness. I commit myself
totally to You. By Your grace, please keep me holy in my spirit,
soul and body. I praise You and thank You. In Jesus' Name,
AMEN!!

If you are married, ask God to heal the marriage
relationship, and have your mate forgive you only if they knew
about it. If the mate doesn't know anything about an
adulterous relationship, you need to personally go to Godly
counseling with your pastor and let him evaluate how to
address that problem.

STEP VI. Rebellion Against God

Many have been in rebellion against God since birth, just for being born into this world.

Consider this question: Say prior to birth in heaven, Jesus came by asking for volunteers to come to earth and live awhile. Would you:

1. Volunteer?
2. If so, would you choose this century or a different one?
3. If you, had your choice, would you:
   * Choose the same parents, exclusive of brutality?
   * Choose your same mother?
   * Choose your same father?
4. Would you be a boy or a girl?
5. Choose your same body?
6. Choose your same face?
7. Choose your mind, character, personality?
8. If you are a woman, are you:
   a. pretty?
   b. attractive?
   c. desirable?
   d. beautiful?
   e. lovable?
9. If you are a man, are you:
   a. handsome?
   b. attractive?
   c. good-looking?
   d. desirable?
10. If Jesus walked up to you right now and gave you a choice, "You can either go with me to heaven right now, or go all the way through life," which way would you choose?

Let's grade ourselves.

To whatever degree you would not volunteer to come to earth, that you would change your century, time of being born, sex; to whatever degree you would not choose your father or mother *under normal circumstances), body, face, mind, character, personality; to whatever degree you have answered these questions in the negative, you are upset with God and you are in spiritual rebellion and angry with Him!

The great commandment is to love the Lord your God with all your heart, mind, soul and strength and love your neighbor as yourself!

Ephesians 2:10(ESV) For we are his workmanship, created in Christ Jesus for good works, which God prepared beforehand, that we should walk in them. If we do not love ourselves, we are dishonoring God.

How would you feel if you bought something special for a child or fixed up the child's room and he said, "I don't like it in there." Would you feel honored or hurt: It would hurt, wouldn't it? If we do not like how we are and how we look, and it's the way God made us, we are dishonoring Him! We are like the child who is given a red wagon and then leaves it out in the rain. If we want to get out of here and back to heaven as fast as we can, we are in rebellion, and angry at who we are and need to be reconciled to being who God created us to be.

Spiritual rebellion sounds like this: "Oh God, I'll never be able to do what you sent me to do. You put me with these people and they are messing me up, and it is not fair!" Anybody ever feel like that?

We must become reconciled to God and learn to love being us, or it will affect us in many ways. It directly affects our relationship to the Father, our ability and confidence to minister to others -- even the ability of our spirit to sustain our health. There are also other reasons people are mad at God, like war, physical handicaps, etc.

Do you want to be healed of all that now?

Pray this prayer aloud:

Dear Heavenly Father, in Jesus' Name I've come to You and confess I have not been too happy with what You have created me to be. I've been mad at my body because it gets out of shape! I've been mad at my mind because it doesn't remember things. I have been disgusted and disgruntled at my situations --- some of it directed at my parents. I've looked at others and coveted their looks and family situations. I have been upset.

I have not even realized I have been committing sin and rebellion against You! I did not understand that when You put me in my family, You intended to bring forth glory out of those conditions that could not have been done any other way. I did

39

not have proper trust in You. I lost that part and I confess that fact today.

I admit I have been in spiritual rebellion. I've resisted my own body. I have not been able to love my brothers and sisters, mate and family as I should. Lord, I want to be reconciled to my proper time and place, so forgive me for my ignorance.

Your Word says that people perish for lack of knowledge, and I recognize that some of this is flesh and some of it is caused by allowing a spirit of rebellion to come in and rule my thoughts. Father, forgive me for hurting You.

Now, Satan, in Jesus' Name, I bind up the spirit of rebellion, according to Matthew 18:18, cast it out and call in a humble and contrite spirit and the Spirit of God!

And now dear Father, I want to be reconciled to You and to being myself. Forgive me my rebellion and restore me to fellowship in Jesus' Name. Teach me to love what You are building me into, so I can love being myself and learn to reach out and love others, not in conceit or pride, but in gratitude that I am made in Your image.

I thank You Father, that You are reaching back right now into my past and healing those wounds I have suffered since birth. You whisper to me, "'I did not make anyone else like you --- nobody else has a voice like yours; even your finger prints are unique. Just as no two snowflakes are the same, I made you to be my unique glory, and I love you just as you are'."

Thank You, Jesus. Amen.

STEP VII. Wounded Spirit

We need to see that our human spirits can sin, not in the Holy Spirit, but our human spirit. *Psalm 32:2 says, "Blessed is the man against whom the Lord counts no iniquity(evil minded), and in whose spirit there is no deceit."*

Psalm 51:10-12: "Create in me a clean heart, oh God, and renew a right spirit within me, cast me not away from your presence; and take not your Holy Spirit from me. Restore to me the joy of your salvation; and uphold me with a willing spirit." There is no need for a new and right spirit if there is nothing wrong with the old one.

Ezekiel 36:26: "And I will give you a new heart, and a new spirit I will put within you. And I will remove the heart of stone from your flesh and give you a heart of flesh."
Ezekiel 11:19: "And I will give them one heart, and a new spirit I will put within them. I will remove the heart of stone from their flesh and give them a heart of flesh."

First, the Father wants to put a new spirit, a right spirit, within us, and later He says He will put His Spirit (the Holy Spirit) within us, but He wants to clean us up first. In *2Corinthians 7:1Paul, writing to Christians, says, "Since we have these promises, beloved, let us cleanse ourselves from every defilement of body and spirit, bringing holiness to completion in the fear of God."*

James 4:5: Or do you suppose it is to no purpose that Scripture says, "He yearns jealously over the spirit he has made to dwell within us?" So you see we can and do sin in our own personal spirit. *Sin here is regarded as making wrong choices. Psalm 58:3 says that, "the wicked are estranged from the womb; they go astray from birth, speaking lies."*

Isaiah 48:8: "For I knew you would surely deal treacherously, and that from before birth you were called a rebel."

James 2:26: "For as the body apart from the spirit is dead." (This refers to our own personal spirit.)

Job 32:8: "But it is the spirit in man, the breath of the Almighty, that makes him understand."

So we know we have understanding in our spirits --- not just in our minds. Samples of experiences in our spirits:

Troubledness - *John 13:21: After saying these things, Jesus was troubled in his spirit, and testified, and said, "Truly, truly I say to you, one of you will betray me."*

Distress - *Acts 17:16: Now, while Paul waited for them at Athens, his spirit was provoked within him as he saw that the city was full of idols.*

Fear - *2Timothy 1:7: "For God gave us a spirit not of fear but of power and love and self- control." Longing in our spirits. Isaiah 26:9--"My soul yearns for you in the night; my spirit within me earnestly seeks you. For when your judgments are in the earth, the inhabitants of the world learn righteousness."*

Our spirits testify - *Romans 8:16-17: "The Spirit himself bears witness that we are children of God, and if children, then heirs-heirs of God and fellow heirs with Christ, provided we suffer with him in order that we also may be glorified with him."*

Prayer - *1 Corinthians 14:14: "For if I pray in a tongue, my spirit prays but my mind is unfruitful."*

Song - *1 Corinthians 14:15: "What am I to do? I will pray with my spirit, but I will pray with my mind also; I will sing with my spirit, but I will sing with my mind also."*

Praise –*1 Corinthians 14:16: "Otherwise, if you give thanks with your spirit, how can anyone in the position of an outsider say, "Amen" to your thanksgiving when he does not know what you are saying?"*

Tendency toward envy - *James 4:5: "Or do you suppose it is to no purpose that Scripture says, "He yearns jealously over the spirit he has made to dwell within us?"*

Unfaithfulness - *Psalm 78:8: "And that they should not be like their fathers, a stubborn and rebellious generation, a generation whose heart was not steadfast, whose spirit was not faithful to God."*

Our spirit worships - *John 4:23-24: "But the hour is coming, when the true worshippers shall worship the Father in spirit and in truth, for the Father seeking such people to worship Him. God is a Spirit, and those that worship Him must worship in spirit and truth."*

John the Baptist leaps in Elizabeth's womb when Mary comes to visit. *(*Luke 1:41-44*).* He was alive in his spirit; there was understanding in his spirit; he perceived and he leapt for joy as he made a reaction to what he perceived in the womb; prayed for their perfect formation, etc.

No wonder Jesus confounded the professors at the age of twelve --- He was educated in the womb of spiritual things.

So, way back we can have been badly hurt. We feel:

1. Rejection from our parents by their attitudes
2. Lack of Love
3. Broken hearts, plus
4. Wounds as we were growing up

In his book, "The Secret Life of the Unborn Child," Dr. Thomas Verney says, "There is no doubt that the child, while in the womb, hears, feels, and experiences what is going on in the environment of the mother. He learns, he makes reactions to what he is learning and he comes out of the womb already pre-disposed to interpret life according to what he experienced in the womb." He talks about character personality, pre-disposition, there are attitudes about the "self" that are already there that tend to color life. He goes on to say, "It isn't just these strong emotions like love and hate that the child will experience, but it's emotions like ambivalence, and for example, like when the parents say, "Oh no --- I'm pregnant!!! --- there's no way we want this child," and then they swing to the other side and say, "Well of course we'll love this child, but how on earth are we going to care for this child? But we'll make it somehow!" That kind of an alternation affects the child and it will come out of the womb with a kind of lethargic personality."

Paula Sandford, whose books on these subjects I've read, said one of their daughters was this way --- she had sort of a sleepy attitude --- not really interested in much of anything, sweet but mellow, no drive. Once they realized the problem, they immediately prayed asking the Lord to heal the wounding she experienced because of their attitudes while carrying her, the anxieties over possibilities of miscarriage, etc., and ambivalence when they first knew she was on the way. Now their daughter is a dynamic young woman, full of drive --- very capable now.

Doctors say that a negative attitude in mothers is extremely damaging to the unborn child --- they give a lot of statistics on how much more frequent is miscarriage where the mother's attitude is negative, how much more frequent there is disease and injury --- how much more frequent is anxiety of heart and personality of a child whose mother had a very negative attitude.

They also say that the baby in the womb reacts to music and responds very positively to music of composers like Mozart, and some become extremely agitated when they hear music by Beethoven, and rock music, because of the loudness --- cymbals, drums, etc., that are startling. They say many mothers who go to concerts have to leave when the music becomes very loud and certain cymbals are used. The babies become so active the mothers are in pain and have to leave and find a quiet place before the child will settle down. This is just to show us that many of us were wounded in our spirits before birth, but praise God, Jesus has the healing for that too!

As we grow up, much happens to hurt us along the way. How it affects us depends largely on our first years of development with our families. Those who were secure, loved and happy could let things bounce off with a shrug. Those who were not, only felt threatened and the hurts were compounded.

A girl made fun of a dress my mother made me in the first grade. That incident changed my whole personality. I became an extrovert to prove I was somebody. Later in life, the enemy used this same person to hurt me even deeper. From there came rejection, hurt, anger, bitterness, unforgiveness and rebellion against all men and suspicion against women. In the same way a snowball rolling down the hill gathers more snow, plus any other debris in its path, hurts --- sexual abuse, especially by members of our family --- affect our lives today unless death with. Many of us can identify with what is being said here. Old things cannot pass away and have all things become new until old things are healed and forgiven. As long as the sliver is in the sore, it continues to fester, right?

You need to ask Jesus to walk back with you and heal you once and for all. If you are wondering about your children and your attitudes when you were carrying them, you need to do this: After you have received healing, share with them what you have learned. Ask them to pray with you a simple prayer of forgiveness and healing for THEM that I will give you when we are finished. Also have them pray the prayer to break

44

generational curses for themselves. You can lead the younger ones through it, (ages 4 to 8)

Pray this prayer aloud:

Dear Heavenly Father, thank You for Your tender mercies. Thank You for Jesus, as I come to You in His precious Name. Father, I believe I've been wounded in my spirit from the womb, and right now I want it to go on record that I forgive my parents for this, because they had no more idea than I did how much the unborn child is alive and aware. I ask You now to forgive me for my lack of knowledge and release me from my anguish as I release my parents (living or deceased). Heal my children as you are healing me, and I will be obedient to share with them what I have learned here. Lord Jesus, I am asking You to identify with me in my hurts of rejection, for You experienced rejection in a hideous way and can understand my anguish. Heal my wounds of rejection, hopelessness, inadequacies, craving for love, and even the effects of the turmoil my parents were going through that filled me with anxieties and fears from birth.

Come in, Lord Jesus, and close those wounds, filling them with the balm of Gilead.

And now, Satan, I REBUKE you from my past, up to the present, and I bind you and all your evil spirits that were assigned to me and mine, according to Matthew 18:18, commanding you to go, Go, GO in Jesus' Name. I break your power and recover myself out of the snare of the devil, and I loose ministering angels to come fill me with the love of God. Holy Spirit, fill me to overflowing with your Spirit oh God, a humble and contrite spirit, the unspeakable "joy of the Lord", the "garment of praise" for the spirit of heaviness, the oil of gladness and loving, forgiving, compassion for each other in Jesus. Oh glory--- I'm set free! **Thank You, thank You, Jesus!**

Here is a prayer for your children. Go see them, write, call, etc. In prayer walk back together. Go back to the womb and ask them--- "Will you forgive us if we allowed our concerns to cause you to feel unwanted when we first heard the news?" I/we loved you when you came, and long before you were born we changed our feelings, but we want you to forgive us our ignorance of how it may have affected your life."

45

Ask the Lord Jesus to speak into their spirits deep within them and say, *"My child, you are not a mistake. You have a right to be."* Say, *"We want you, we love you, and we thank You, Father, for the gift of _____(child's name)! Thank You, Father, for their lives and the privilege of being their parents. We speak healing to their wounded spirits in Jesus Name.*

VII. GOD'S DREAM FOR US: WALKING IN HEALTH

How To Receive Your Healing
Step 1. The first step to receive miracle healing is to know that the age of miracles has not passed, and that physical healing is part of Christ's ministry today. We need to know that:

A. God is a Healer. Exodus 15:26: saying, "If you will diligently listen to the voice of the Lord your God, and do that which is right in his eyes, and give ear to his commandments and keep all his statutes, I will put none of these diseases on you that I put on the Egyptians, for I am the Lord your healer."

B. He says, "I do not change." *Malachi 3:6a: "For I the Lord do not change."*

C. Jesus Christ healed the sick. *Matthew 9:35:* (teaching, preaching, healing every sickness and every disease among the people). Hebrews 13:8 says that Jesus is the same yesterday, today and forever.

D. Jesus commanded His disciples to heal the sick. Matthew 10:1-8: "And he called to him his twelve disciples and gave them authority over unclean spirits, to cast them out, and to heal every disease and every affliction. The names of the twelve apostles are these: first, Simon, who is called Peter, and Andrew his brother; James the son of Zebedee, and John his brother; Philip and Bartholomew; Thomas and Matthew the tax collector; James the son of Alphaeus, and Thaddaeus; Simon the Zealot, and Judas Iscariot, who betrayed him. These twelve Jesus sent out, instructing them, "Go nowhere among the Gentiles and enter no town of the Samaritans, but go rather to the lost sheep of the house of Israel. And proclaim as you go, saying, 'The kingdom of heaven is at hand.' Heal the sick, raise the dead, cleanse lepers, cast out demons. You received without paying; give without pay."

E. Miracles of healing were everywhere manifested in the ministry of the early church. Acts 3:6-8: "But Peter said, 'I have no silver and gold, but what I do have I give to you. In the name of Jesus Christ of Nazareth, rise up and walk!' And he took him by the right hand and raised him up, and immediately his feet and ankles were made strong. And he leaping up he stood and began to walk, and entered the temple with them walking and leaping and praising God." Hebrews 2:3-4: "How shall we escape if we neglect such a great salvation? It was declared first by the Lord, and it was attested to us by those who heard, while God also bore witness by signs and wonders and various miracles and by gifts of the Holy Spirit distributed according to his will." Matthew 28:20: ...."I am with you always, to the end of the age."Read and study these scriptures.

F. Jesus commissioned all believers among all nations, to the end of the world, to cast out devils and to lay hands on the sick, promising they will recover (Mark 16:15-20).

Miracle healing was first administered through the spoken Word of Jehovah God, then through the ministry of the Lord, Jesus Christ. Next through His disciples, who acted on His Word and followed His example, and later, by the power of the resurrected Christ and Holy Spirit being manifest through the early Church, and last, by the same risen Christ and power of the same Holy Spirit functioning through the lives of all believers in the world today. So the age of miracles has not passed--- physical healing is still as much a part of Christ's ministry today as it ever was.

Step 2: The second step to receiving healing is **to know God's promises to heal in the scriptures**, and to be convinced that they are for you personally.

a. Reading the Bible, His Word, is the same as if He were here speaking to you personally.

b. You can't separate God from His Word. He is not only in it and part of it, but He's behind it and He watches over it to perform it (Jer. 1:12). Jesus said, "Truly, truly, I say to you, whoever believes in me will do the works that I do; and greater works that these will he do, because I am going to the Father. Whatever you ask in my name, this I will do, that the Father may be glorified in the Son. If you ask me anything in my name,

I will do it." Anything includes healing, and that means you! Mark 16:17-18: "And these signs will accompany those that believe...they will lay their hands on the sick, and they will recover." "They shall recover" is Christ's promise to everyone who is sick, without exception. Jesus said, "Only believe," to an anguished father whose daughter was dead, and Jesus raised her! Mark 5:35-36, 41-42: "While he was still speaking, there came from the ruler's house some who said, 'Your daughter is dead. Why trouble the Teacher any further?' But overhearing what they said, Jesus said, "Do not fear, only believe"...Taking her by the hand he said to her, "Talithacumi,' which means little girl, I say to you, arise." And immediately the girl got up and began walking (for she was twelve years of age), and they were immediately overcome with amazement.

Step 3: The third step to receiving healing is to understand that God wants you to be well--- only Satan wants you to suffer. Acts 10:38: "Jesus...went about doing good and healing **all** who were oppressed by the devil..." God created man and woman perfect physically, mentally, and spiritually and put them in the Garden of Eden with material abundance.

Satan introduced sin, sickness and death, as Jesus said of him in John 10:10a: "The thief comes only to steal and kill and destroy." Our physical beauty and health has been scarred with every form of disease. In spite of medical achievements, immunizations to halt certain diseases, man still hasn't been able to find a cure for the common cold, let alone cancer.

The Good News is the Gospel. Isaiah 53:4-5 tells of God's plan to send Jesus: "Surely he has borne our griefs, and carried our sorrows...and with His wounds we are healed."Isaiah 61:1 and Luke 4: "The spirit of the Lord God is upon me. Because the Lord has anointed me to bring good news to the poor; he has sent me to bind up the brokenhearted, to proclaim liberty to the captives, and the opening of the prison to those who are bound."

Step 4: The fourth step to receiving healing is to understand that physical healing is a part of salvation. (The Greek word "sozo" means saved from hell healed of all diseases and delivered from the power of Satan.)

a. Do you enjoy seeing your children suffer? Of course not. Neither does the Heavenly Father.

b. We are invited to come boldly into the throne of grace (unmerited favor). (Hebrews 4:16)

c. God says in Jeremiah 33:3, "Call to Me and I will answer you..." Jesus says, "If you abide in Me, and My words abide in you, ask whatever you wish, and it will be done for you." (John 15:7) He also said, in John 14:14, "If you ask Me anything in My name, I will do it." And 1 Peter 3:12 says, "For the eyes of the Lord are on the righteous, and His ears are open to their prayers..." 1 John 5:14-15 says, "And this is the confidence that we have toward Him, that if we ask anything according to His will (or according to His promises), He hears us. And if we know that He hears us in whatever we ask, we know that we have the requests that we have asked of Him." Matthew 7:8a-- For everyone who asks, receives." All these promises are contingent on being righteous--- walking in fellowship with Him, not sinning!

The foundation for answered prayer is to realize that the only reason you can expect any blessing from God is that Jesus died to provide that blessing. We must be sure what we are praying for is provided for by Christ's death. In other words, some people want healing "because they have suffered so much," or "because they are a good, sincere person," or "because they have been faithful to the church." None of these reasons are valid to receive healing from Christ.

The only worthy foundation on which to base our faith for healing is that He Himself took our infirmities and bore our sickness. Certainly He carried our diseases and suffered our pains. "...AND WITH HIS WOUNDS WE ARE HEALED." (Isaiah 53:5b) In His death He provided every blessing man could desire or require. We must look to the cross where the price was paid for the blessing we seek. He died to provide it; it does belong to us. And He wants us to have it. Claim it boldly.

Step 6: The sixth step to receiving healing is to believe when you pray that you have received what you asked for. This step is called "faith."

a. Faith means you're convinced that what God promised and what you asked for is yours; that you have

49

received it (even before you can see it or feel it). This kind of faith is based on God's promise alone. Believers should say, "If God says it, then it is true." "If God's Word says, By His stripes I'm healed, I'm healed." Faith says, "I have it now. It is written; it is mine. Praise the Lord."

To walk by faith is to give God's Word the preeminence over our senses. 2 Corinthians 5:7: "For we walk by faith, not by sight." Romans 4:17b says, "God...called into existence the things that do not exist." Man says, "Seeing is believing." That is being a doubting Thomas. God says, "Believe you receive it when you pray and you shall have it."

Faith for healing is exactly the same as faith for salvation. God's Word says the sinner is to believe he is saved, confess his salvation boldly and on the basis of God's promise alone, even before he feels the joy of forgiveness. The joy will come if he will believe and claim the gift by faith. He must believe on the authority of God's Word alone that he is saved. This is also the way God heals sick bodies and fulfills any of His redemptive promises.

The Bible tells us God's Word does not return to Him void; but shall accomplish that which it was sent to do. Isaiah 55:11: "So shall My word be that goes out from My mouth, it shall not return to me empty, but it shall accomplish that which I purpose, and shall succeed in the thing for which I sent it."

To learn how to believe that God hears and answers us when we pray is a great blessing in itself, because you can learn to pray the prayer of faith scores of times for yourself and others, and your whole life can be spent knowing the joy of having your prayers answered and promises fulfilled by God Himself. Be sure God hears your prayers by checking to see if you're in right standing. A quick prayer for cleansing (from a sincere heart) is all it takes. I John 1:9: "If we confess our sins, He is faithful and just to forgive us our sins, and to cleanse us from all unrighteousness."

To receive healing after you get sick is great, but to live in divine health continually is greater. And the key to both lies within the Word of God. In fact, Proverbs 4:22 says that God's words are life to us and medicine to our flesh. The following prayer is full of those precious words. Use it to help build the image of divine health in your heart and to activate the faith within you. Speak it often with confidence, knowing that God watches over His Word to perform it (Jer. 1:12).

PRAY THIS PRAYER

Father, in the name of Jesus, I confess Your Word concerning healing. As I do this, I believe and say that Your Word will not return to You void, but will accomplish what it says it will. Therefore, I believe in the name of Jesus that I am healed according to 1 Peter 2:24.

It is written in Your Word that Jesus Himself took my infirmities and bore my sicknesses (Matt. 8:17). Therefore, with great boldness and confidence, I say on the authority of that written Word that I am redeemed from the curse of sickness, and I refuse to tolerate its symptoms.

Satan, I speak to you in the name of Jesus and say that your principalities, powers, your master spirits who rule the present darkness, and your spiritual wickedness in heavenly places are bound from operating against me in any way. I am loosed from your assignment. I am the property of Almighty God, and I give you no place in me. I dwell in the secret place of the Most High God; I abide, remain stable and fixed under the shadow of the Almighty, whose power no foe can withstand (Ps. 91:1).

Now Father, because I reverence and worship You, I have the assurance of Your Word that the angel of the Lord encamps around me and delivers me from every evil work. No evil shall befall me, no plague or calamity shall come near my dwelling (Ps. 91:10).

I confess that the Word of God abides in me and delivers to me perfect soundness of mind and wholeness in body and spirit from the deepest parts of my nature, even to the joints and marrow of my bones (Heb. 4:12). Your Word is medication and life to my flesh for the law of the Spirit of Life operates in me and makes me free from the law of sin and death (Rom. 8:2).

I have on the whole armor of God and the shield of faith protects me from all the fiery darts of the wicked (Eph. 6:16). Jesus is the High Priest of my confession, and I hold fast to my confession of faith in Your Word (Heb. 3:1). I stand immovable and fixed in the full assurance that I have health and healing NOW, in Jesus' name.

HEALING AFFIRMATIONS

1. I give to You, Father, my total mind, spirit, body and emotions.
2. The healing light of Jesus Christ is flowing through my mind renewing and restoring my thought (conscious and subconscious) to be in alignment with His thoughts.
3. The healing love of Jesus Christ is flowing through my spirit, mending and healing and creating a new heart within me.
4. The fruit of the Holy Spirit is becoming evident through my emotions and soul, with love, joy, peace, patience, kindness, goodness, faithfulness, gentleness and self-control.
5. My physical body is being totally filled with the living water and light of Jesus Christ in every cell and tissue, every nerve and bone, and every internal organ.
6. I give to You, Lord Jesus, my immune system, which You created to be 5 times more powerful than anything in this world, to cooperate with Your healing touch to bring about perfect healing.
7. My total being is cooperating and working with Jesus Christ in me, to bring harmony and balance and perfect peace.
8. Belief, trust and faith are a natural part of my thoughts, my speech and my actions. Thank You for activating the Word within me, Holy Spirit, and bringing to remembrance, "God sent His Word and healed us".
9. Lord Jesus, You are the light of the world. Your light lives in me. You called me to be the light of the world. I walk in light; therefore, I have perfect health and wonderful fellowship and the blood of Jesus cleanses me.
10. Thank You, Father, for a holy blood transfusion that purifies and cleanses every fiber of my being, causing release, freedom, tranquility and calm.

Proverbs 18:21: Death and life are in the power of the tongue.

***Say these out loud daily till all symptoms are gone. ***

IX. SEVEN WAYS TO RETAIN YOUR HEALING

If we meet the conditions and seek God, He is obligated by His Word to heal us. God cannot lie! *Titus 1:2; Hebrews 6:18: "...with His wounds we are healed." (Isaiah 53:5) "...by His wounds you have been healed." (1 Peter 2:24)* Both of these scriptures speak of your healing as an accomplished fact.

1. Wait on the Lord--- don't be hasty. Be patient! *Isaiah 65:24: "...before they call, I will answer; and while they are yet speaking, I will hear."* Don't give up. Your faith will see you through. Don't waiver.

Don't be double-minded. Don't go by symptoms. The disease is dead, but the body is in recovery! In Mark 11:12-14 Jesus cursed the fig tree. So He has smitten your sickness at the roots. Sometimes He allows the body to go through a period of recovery. Read Mark 16:18--- keep looking up and praising God. Israel shouted before the walls of Jericho fell! God works on "Heavenly Standard Time." One day is as a thousand years, and a thousand years as one day (2 Peter 3: 8-9).

2. Resist the Devil. Satan is a hard loser. Recognize his attempts to counter attack and resist him. James 4:7: "Submit yourselves therefore to God. Resist the devil, and he will flee from you." Luke 11:24, 26: "When the unclean spirit has gone out of a person, it passes through waterless places seeking rest, and finding none it says, 'I will return to my house from which I came.' Then it goes and brings seven other spirits more evil than itself, and they enter and dwell there. And the last state of that person is worse than the first." Mark 4:14-15 & 20, the Parable of the Sower. "The sower sows the word. And these are the ones along the path, where the word is sown: when they hear, Satan immediately comes and takes away the word that is sown in them...But those that were sown on the good soil are the ones who hear the word and accept it and bear fruit, thirtyfold and sixtyfold and a hundredfold." Keep in praise and thanksgiving. Rejoice evermore. Pray without ceasing (intercession until manifestation comes forth). In everything give thanks (1 Thess. 5:16-18). Jesus whipped the devil with the Word. "It is written," Jesus said to the devil and defeated him on the spot! Read Matthew 4:11. Fortify your faith with the Word. The Bible is our sword. Eph. 6:17-- "And

take the helmet of salvation, and sword of the Spirit, which is the word of God."

    3. Give the glory to God. Read the story in Luke 17:11-19 of the ten lepers. Only one gave glory to God. Jesus said to the one, "Rise and go your way; your faith has made you well." "Let them thank the Lord for his steadfast love, for his wondrous works to the children of man!" (Psalm 107:15)
    Maybe you don't feel any better yet. Don't go by feelings; go by faith. Believe God. Take Him at His Word. Faith is believing God will do what He promised to do.
    Shout, "As for me, I believe God, that it shall be even as it was told me." (Acts 27:25) "Bless the Lord, O my soul and forget not all His benefits, Who forgives all your iniquity, Who heals all your diseases." (Psalm 103:2-3)

    4. Go and sin no more. John 5:2-15: "...Sin nor more, that nothing worse may happen to you..." If you were living in sin before your healing, you let the bars down for the entrance of sickness. When you transgress the laws of God, you get in the devil's territory and throw yourself wide open to his malicious attacks. Paul said, "Abstain from every form of evil." (1 Thess. 5:22). Peter said, "Whoever desires to love life and see good days, let him keep his tongue from evil and his lips from speaking deceit; let him turn away from evil and do good..." (1 Peter 3:10-11) The correct environment for one newly healed is one of holiness, not the same corruption and sin he came out of. You can hope to be in health only to the degree that your soul prospers. 3 John 1:2: "Beloved, I pray that all may go well with you and that you may be in good health, as it goes well with your soul." We prosper our souls by filling ourselves with the Word of God.

    5. Consecrate yourself to the Lord. Romans 12:1-2 and present your body a holy living sacrifice. Your new health and strength should be used to glorify Him in His service. Your eyes, ears, hands, feet, tongue and heart should all be consecrated to Christ for service. Romans 6:13 Do not present your members to sin as instruments for unrighteousness, but present yourselves to God as those who have been brought

from death to life, and your members to God as instruments for righteousness

6.Glorify God in your body. 1 Cor. 6:19-20: "Or do you not know that your body is a temple of the Holy Spirit within you, whom you have from God? You are not your own, for you were bought with a price. So glorify God in your body." Don't contaminate your body with harmful things such as alcohol, drugs, late hours, over-work, overeating, etc. We need to use the common sense God gave us and eat properly and rest regularly (Proverbs 23:2). Half of what we eat keeps us alive--- the other half keeps the doctors alive! (1 Cor. 10:31)"So, whether you eat or drink, or whatever you do, do all to the glory of God."

7. "Go...tell them what great things the Lord has done for you." Remember the man with the legion of demons who wanted to go with Jesus after he had been delivered? "Go home to your friends, "Jesus said, "and tell them how much the Lord has done for you, and how He has had mercy on you." Mark 5:19. 2 Tim. 1:8: "Therefore do not be ashamed of the testimony about our Lord..." Yes, if you want to keep your healing, go and tell others. Magnify the Name of the Lord!!

My prayer for you reading this is: "Now may the God of peace himself sanctify you completely, and may your whole spirit and soul and body be kept blameless at the coming of our Lord Jesus Christ." Amen. (1 Thess. 5:23)

Our authority over the enemy. 1 John 3:8b: "The reason the Son of God appeared was to destroy the works of the devil."

In Luke 10:19, Jesus said, "Behold, I have given you authority to tread on serpents and scorpions, and over all the power of the enemy, and nothing shall hurt you." Authority is delegated power.

A policeman directing traffic has authority to stop cars by raising his hands. But he doesn't have the physical power to stop them. What could one man do? He couldn't hold back a car with his physical strength. A policeman doesn't use his strength; he uses the authority given him by the government, city or state that he serves. We can step right out in front of the devil, hold up our hand, and tell him not to come any further; using our authority, because Jesus delegated that authority to us!

Please read the first three chapters of Ephesians. Paul prayed spirit-anointed prayers for the church at Ephesus, and those prayers belong to us too, since they were given by the Holy Spirit.

Read Eph. 1:16-19. We need to ask God to give unto us a spirit of wisdom and revelation knowledge. Eph. 3:14-17: "For this reason I bow my knees unto the Father, from whom every family in heaven and on earth is named, that according to the riches of His glory he may grant to be strengthened with power through His Spirit in the inner being so that Christ may dwell within your hearts through faith...:

Brother Kenneth Hagen said the turning point in his life came by praying these prayers over and over for six months, and revelation of God's Word began to come. He began to see things in the Word he had not seen before. He said he learned more in six months about the Bible than he had learned in fourteen years as a pastor and sixteen years as a Christian.

Eph. 6:12 says, "For we do not wrestle against flesh and blood, but against the rulers, against the authorities, against the cosmic powers over this present darkness, against the spiritual forces of evil in heavenly places." And praise the Lord! We have authority over this. Thank You, Jesus!

Eph. 1:3: "Blessed be the God and Father of our Lord Jesus Christ, who has blessed us in Christ with every spiritual blessing in the heavenly places." All spiritual blessings means Christ has already made every provision for us. They belong to us. But if we don't know it or use them, they're lost.

It's as if we have a joint bank account with our Heavenly Father, and never write a check. We often read in the papers about a person with lots of money who dies in poverty. They live in squalor, eating out of garbage cans, with a mattress stuffed full of money.

It's like packages under the Christmas tree left unopened; or the man on the ship who nearly starves to death eating cheese and crackers, not realizing until time to land that meals were included in the price of his ticket! We must use what belongs to us. Eph. 6:10 "Finally, be strong in the Lord and in the strength of His might." We're supernatural people.

In Luke 10:19 Jesus gave us power over all power of the enemy. He said in John 10:10, "The thief comes only to steal and kill and destroy. I came that they may have life and have it abundantly."

Sickness and disease comes from Satan, but Acts 10:38 states, "...God anointed Jesus of Nazareth with the Holy Spirit and with power. He went about doing good and healing all who were oppressed by the devil, for God was with him."

Matt. 8:16-17: "That evening they brought to Him many who were oppressed by demons, and He cast out the spirits with a word and healed all who were sick. This was to fulfill what was spoken by the prophet Isaiah: He took our illnesses and bore our diseases."

So now...

Jesus passed onto us the authority to use His Name and carry on His work Mark 16:15-20. Jesus said, "In My Name they will cast out demons...they will lay their hands on the sick, and they will recover."

Facts:

1. Sickness is not any more natural than sin. God made all things "very good". We were created healthy, strong, happy, made to fellowship with God.

2. Sin and sickness came into the world through the fall. Jesus heals both!

3. God made a covenant with His children at first to take sickness from among them if they would serve Him. Later it became a continual finding of them in sickness and pestilence because they were not serving Him, but worshipping idols. Eventually they would turn to God for forgiveness and their sicknesses were healed. Exodus 23:25: "You shall serve the LORD your God, and he will bless your bread and your water, and I will take sickness away from among you."

4. Everyone who looked at the brazen serpent was healed then--- everyone who looks to Jesus today can be healed today. The brazen serpent represented Jesus.

5. Everyone was commanded to do his own looking then--- everyone is commanded to do his own believing today.

6. Since their curse was removed by lifting up a "type" of Calvary, our curse was certainly removed by Calvary itself.

7. Sickness came directly from Satan. Job 2:7:"So Satan went out from the presence of the Lord and struck Job with loathsome sores from the sole of his foot to the crown of his head." Job maintained steadfast faith as he cried out to God for deliverance, and he was healed.

Luke 13:11-13 & 16 says that Jesus cast out a spirit of infirmity from a woman bound by Satan, and she was healed. In Matthew 12:22, there was a man possessed of the devil who was blind and dumb. Jesus healed him, insomuch that the blind and dumb spoke and saw! Mark 9:17-26, a demon was the cause of a boy being deaf and dumb with confusions. Jesus cast out the demon, and the boy was healed. Jesus always treated sin, disease and devils the same:
He rebuked them all. He was manifested to destroy the works of the devil.

The right to pray and receive an answer is given every believer. John 14:14:"If you ask me anything in my name, I will do it." This logically includes asking for healing if one is sick.

When people question if it's God's will to heal, how is it that they will do everything in their human skills to get healed, whether they think it's God's will or not? If it's not God's will it would be wrong to seek healing, but if it is God's will, then all healing is from God, whether one recovers from aid of medical science or by prayer and faith in God's promises.

Therefore, if we are going on God's promises, we have to step out in faith and begin to do what the Word says, for...

If we let Satan get us to regret yesterday and worry about tomorrow, he has completely ruined today.

Here is how to keep your healing: When the enemy tries to steal your joy, healing or freedom, speak God's Word over your body. When the enemy tries to steal your joy, healing or freedom, speak God's Word over your body.

Psalm 103:2-5, 12--"Bless the Lord, O my soul, and forget not all his benefits, Who forgives all my iniquity and heals all my diseases, Who redeems my life from the pit, Who crowns me with steadfast love and mercy, Who satisfies me with good so that my youth is renewed like the eagle's. As far as the east is from the west, so far does He removed our transgressions from us."

Proverbs 4:20-22: "My son, be attentive to my words; incline your ear to my sayings. Let them not escape from your sight; keep them within your heart. For they are life to those who find them, and healing to all their flesh."

Matthew 8:16-17: "That evening they brought to him many who were oppressed by demons, and he cast out the spirits with a word and healed all who were sick. This was to fulfill what was spoken by the prophet Isaiah: 'He took our illnesses and bore our diseases.'

1 Peter 2:24: "He himself bore our sins in his body on the tree, that we might die to sin and live to righteousness. By his wounds you are healed."

Psalm 91:14-16: God speaks: "Because he holds fast to Me in love, I will deliver him; I will protect him, because he knows My name. When he calls to Me, I will answer him; I will be with him in trouble; I will rescue him and honor him. With long life I will satisfy him and show him My salvation."

Mark 16:15-18: "Go into all the world and proclaim the gospel to the whole creation. Whoever believes and is baptized will be saved, but whoever does not believe will be condemned. And these signs will accompany those who believe: in My name they will cast out demons; they will speak in new tongues; they will pick up serpents with their hands; and if they drink any deadly poison, it will not hurt them; they will lay their hands on the sick, and they will recover."

James 5:14-16: "Is any sick among you? Let him call for the elders of the church, and let them pray over him, anointing him with oil in the name of the Lord. And the prayer of faith shall save the one who is sick, and the Lord shall raise him up.And if he has committed sins, he will be forgiven. Therefore, confess your sins to one another and pray for one another, that you may be healed. The prayer of a righteous person has great power as it is working."

James 4:7: "Submit yourselves therefore to God. Resist the devil, and he will flee from you."

Psalm 116: "I love the Lord, because He has heard my voice and my pleas for mercy.

Because He inclined His ear to me, therefore I will call on him as long as I live.

The snares of death encompass me, the pangs of Sheol laid hold on me; I suffered distress and anguish. Then I called on the name of the Lord: 'O Lord, I pray, deliver my soul!'

Gracious is the Lord, and righteous; our God is merciful.

The Lord preserves the simple; when I was brought low, He saved me. Return, O my soul, to your rest; for the Lord has dealt bountifully with you. For you have delivered my soul from death, my eyes from tears, my feet from stumbling; I will walk before the Lord in the land of the living. I believed, even when I spoke: 'I am greatly afflicted', I said in my alarm, 'All mankind are liars'.

What shall I render to the Lord for all His benefits to me? I will lift up the cup of salvation and call on the name of the Lord, I will pay my vows to the Lord in the presence of all His people.

Precious in the sight of the Lord is the death of His saints.

Oh Lord, I am Your servant; I am Your servant, the son of Your maidservant. You have loosed my bonds. I will offer to You the sacrifice of thanksgiving and call on the name of the Lord.

I will pay my vow to the Lord in the presence of all His people, in the courts of the house of the Lord, in your midst, O Jerusalem. Praise the Lord!"

Proverbs 23:7a: "For he is like one who is inwardly calculating..." See yourself well.

Matthew 12:34b: "...for out of the abundance of the heart the mouth speaks." Confess you are recovering.

Isaiah 57:19: "Creating the fruit of the lips. 'Peace, peace, to the far and the near,' says the Lord, 'And I will heal him." Speak positive.

Luke 8:12: "The ones along the path are those who have heard; then the devil comes and takes away the word from their hearts, so that they may not believe and be saved." (Greek "sozo"). Don't let the devil steal what is rightfully yours!

James 1:5-9, 12: "If any of you lacks wisdom, let him ask God, who gives generously to all without reproach, and it will be given him. But let him ask in faith, with no doubting, for the one who doubts is like a wave of the sea that is driven and tossed by the wind. For that person must not suppose that he will receive anything from he Lord; he is a double-minded man, unstable in all his ways. Blessed is the man who remains steadfast under trial, for when he has stood the test he will receive the crown of life, which God has promised to those who love Him."

Eph. 6:10-14a: "Finally, be strong in the Lord and in the strength of His might. Put on the whole armor of God, that you may be able to stand against the schemes of the devil. For we wrestle not against flesh and blood, but against the rulers, against the authorities, against the cosmic powers over this present darkness, against spiritual forces of evil in the heavenly places. Therefore take up the whole armor of God, that you may be able to withstand in the evil day, and having done all (all you know to do), to stand firm. Stand therefore....."

I want it understood that this is not a formula, special method, or the only way to minister healing and deliverance. It is simply the way the Holy Spirit has taught me. Also, each case that I minister to is different and handled in a different way. However, the basics are still true. We must be in right standing ourselves with God before we minister to anyone for any reason, and the prayers are always the same for the different steps--- at least for me.

If I have been of some help--- praise the Lord and God bless you.

Evelyn Diment

Lively Hope Ministries
P.O. Box 821961
Vancouver, WA 98682

www.livelyhope.org

APPENDIX
WORKSHEET A

People who have hurt me!

People that I have hurt!

Sins, bondages & problems I am struggling with now!

I praise the mercy of the Lord and thank Rev. Evelyn Diment for delivering me from the spirit of bondage--- namely alcohol--- and for Rev. Diment's continued love and support.

I was on my way to destruction and death from alcohol abuse, had it not been for this intervention. There were many warning signals as I was growing up in a tight-knit ethnic environment. My father, grandfather, and a host of relatives were alcoholics, so alcohol was just a natural way of life in my young and adult life. As a teenager, I was allowed to drink with the family at special occasions and found my body readily accepting and liking the effects. Little did I know that those "minute highs" would grasp my inner being and not release me, causing me, my husband and small son tremendous grief. I was able to handle my drinking till after my son was born, at which time I started experiencing more stress than I could handle. I turned to alcohol for release, and as the months and years passed I became hopelessly addicted. Once a month I would experience a two/three day drinking binge and then be sober and guilty for the remainder of the month--- till next month, when any minor experience would set me off again.

Towards the end of my drinking career, my binges became longer and I knew I would not be able to survive my last binge of seven days, but I also knew I could "never" give up drinking. My body emaciated and my mind in a panic, I started calling local churches for prayer--- for help. From polite responses like, "Call back when you're sober," to curt prayers and good-byes, I was led into desperation. I didn't want death, I wanted life, but where? In one last ditch effort, I miraculously got the phone number of Evelyn from her publishing house in Oklahoma and called her.

She offered me help! After talking with me and giving me assurance, understanding, love and prayers, we made a date to meet the very next morning. With my body in horrid withdrawal, tremendous pain and tremor, I drove to her home--- only by the grace of God! I spent the whole morning with her, from running back and forth to the bathroom in the beginning to prayer and deliverance. When I left her home, I was a new person! I experienced no more withdrawal and there was instant relief from tremors and pain. I left with hope for a future with my family and life with Christ.

It has now been three years of freedom from alcohol. There has not been a day since that I have desired a drink. The Lord removed total desire and replaced it with a whole and healthy body and sound mind, and with each passing month and year a closer walk with Him.

Thank you,
Sonia Brikner

~~~~~~

I have had rheumatoid arthritis for 4 years. During this time I have struggled with the pain, change in lifestyle, and fear of the drugs I must take, as well as what the future will bring. These classes have given me hope that I don't have to put up with this disease. I have been healed by the Holy Spirit and look forward to feeling the results in the next few weeks (or days!). I have also noted a sense of healing my relationship with my husband. Also, I have noticed a peace with my children. I'm much more patient and less likely to blow up at them. More than anything, I've noticed a sense of security--- a confidence in Him, especially with the twice daily prayers of protection and Armor of God. I've been eager to get into the Word and claim His promises of healing.

Connie Johnson
Note: Since this was written, Connie came to class (Breakthrough) and gave the following testimony:

I was taking a shower a few days ago, thanking and praising the Lord for His goodness and what He is doing in my life, when He spoke to me and told me I could bend my knees! I very carefully tried one knee and then the other. I was thrilled. I ran out of the shower screaming at my husband, who was still in bed, "Look--- look what the Lord has done!" I bent my knees and went up and down clear to the floor. I hadn't been able to bend them for 2 years, and if I was on the floor, I couldn't get up. Now I can do it all. Thank you Jesus!

~~~~~~~~~~~~~~~~~~~~~~~~~~~~~~~~~~~~~~~

I've had very bad allergies and asthma for the past 3 years, since moving from Wisconsin. I haven't been able to be outside the house for more than 15 minutes without developing a bad headache. My medical treatment involved getting allergy shots every 4 or 5 days, using nasal sprays and inhalers 4 times every day, as well as taking pills twice a day.

On Feb. 17, 1990, I prayed all the prayers to cast out spirit of infirmity, after listening to Evelyn's Breakthrough tapes. After attending her last 2 classes, we again prayed and I was anointed with oil. Four days later my breathing tests were normal and a medical test to evaluate my nose was the best ever. Since then I have been able to stop all my pills and shots, and my allergies and asthma are completely gone

Travis, age 11, has been our adopted son for 2 years. He has had a very difficult time being obedient and has had uncontrollable anger. He has not wanted deliverance. My husband and I waited until he was ready and we all prayed together (the prayers in the Freedom Now book) for his deliverance. Since then, he has had no uncontrollable anger, and his resentment toward his mom (me) is gone. Praise God!

My mom has terminal cancer, which has been getting worse. The doctors have only a very few treatments left to help her. She prayed with me over the telephone to cast out the spirit of infirmity and since then, after just one treatment, her x-rays have shown improvement! She has had very few bad side effects from her treatment, and the pain she was having, her shortness of breath, and her coughing have left. Sometimes she still has pain, but the root has been cast out. It will leave permanently in God's timing. She is coming from the East Coast for the Breakthrough Seminar to receive the rest of what God has for her.

Ellen Stroud

~~~~~~

I just wanted to let you know how much your prayers were appreciated...I am healed of cancer. The doctor just can't seem to believe it, as they said it was all through my body. But as you know, there is nothing impossible with the Lord, and if you have faith, I know He will help you. The doctor had me come back for a check-up. I told them they wouldn't find any cancer, for I had been healed and the cancer taken out of my body by the Lord. They didn't believe it, but after my test and they found no cancer in my body they were surprised...As we know He healed people while He was here on the earth...He is the same Lord and can heal today...Thanks again for helping me get healed.

Love,
Effie Clay

~~~~~~

      In October of 1988 I began to attend East Hill. I was in a confused, desperate state of mind, believing that Jesus could and would help me with my troubles, fears, hurts and addiction, but not sure where I could find the acceptance I needed. After hearing Pastor Ted, I knew that East Hill was the place I was looking for. The grace of God was so evident to me that I continued coming. In January I gathered my courage and attended my first Freedom Now Class. I was amazed at the response. It was as though Jesus was talking to me right through those people! I fit in, felt accepted and could find real answers. I prayed the prayers of deliverance and went to counseling for inner healing. I have since learned more about the grace of God and staying free. God has restored relationships in my life that I thought were hopeless. I am free from drug addiction and have no desire to return. I am learning on a continuous basis to turn to the Word of God and His ways of dealing with life. I know that my old ways of responding to my situations were wrong. I was powerless to change on my own I'm now learning to see myself and situations through different eyes. I feel like someone removed the blindfolds and now I see a whole new world. My heart feels secure. I have hope for a bright new future, with no fear and dread of what's going to happen tomorrow.

<div align="right">
Vickie Anderson
</div>

~~~~~~

I first knew that I was an alcoholic in 1986, but did not recognize that alcoholism was a spirit of bondage manifesting itself in a bottle. I now know why in 1987, my first year without alcohol, did not set me free from that bondage. When Evelyn prayed the prayer of deliverance with me in March of 1989, I felt the first sense of relief from that terrible spirit. It took me three years to find that relief could be had very simply in a single day, through prayer and asking God for help.

The lesson I learned that fateful day was that while alcoholism certainly manifests itself as a physical mental problem, it is first and foremost a spiritual disease, and the solution is spiritual.

Neal Ballard

~~~~~~~~~~~~~~~~~

Dear Evelyn,

Many wonderful blessings have happened for my husband and me since attending your Breakthrough seminar last spring. The miracles and changes in our lives really are too numerous to express on this sheet of paper!

First of all, after the seminar itself, we woke up the next Sunday morning and jumped out of bed to start reading and soaking in the literature you sent home with us. As we sat down, we looked at each other with big smiles. I said to my husband, "I feel like this is the first day I've been born! I feel like it's a new beginning." My husband said, "I was just feeling the same way---- all squeaky clean!"

Anyway, that was the start. Since then the Lord has begun a precious healing process in me. We had a head-on car accident 8 years ago and I've suffered with several things wrong with both my inner ears as a result. I had dizziness, balance problems, black-outs at times, loud noises in my ears, nausea---- the list could go on, but that's not the point! The point is that God has restored my balance to perfection! He has taken away any dizziness and problems with movement of any sort. And the problems that I still am facing don't come every single day and many times each day. They're becoming farther apart! Praise the Lord!

The other miracles are just as big. The healing of a very, very poor, almost crippling, self- image was done. What a relief to accept myself after 30-some years of hating who I was! And relationships healed that I didn't even know were so out of balance---- like they were just supposed to "be that way!" What a joke and deceitful lie!

The list could go on, as I said before, and I glory and praise my God for His incredible, awesome love and faithfulness. The challenge now is to continue in the renewing of my mind and staying clean. Sometimes that is much easier said than done because of listening and believing old tapes that want to keep me as the "old creature". But bless the Lord, I continue on, believing that my healing is here and it's expressing itself as wholeness in me every morning.

I hope I haven't rattled on, Evelyn! I really have so much more I could say, but somehow this has ended up on the paper! I'll write more after this next class and finish the story!! Plus, Elizabeth will write too!

Thank you so much, dear friend, for your outpouring of love, encouragement and wisdom. It has been life-changing through our Lord Jesus. I love you!

Love in Christ,
Shelley Long

~~~~~~~~~~~~~~~~~

Chronic Fatigue Syndrome-maybe that is what I have, I thought to myself. There has to be a reason for all of this tiredness and lethargy. I was so weary that it scared me. I didn't know whether to be upset or relieved when my doctor could find nothing physically wrong with me. It could be depression he suggested and wanted to prescribe something, but I wanted to be sure before going on any medication and consulted a Christian psychiatrist. He gave me an MRI psychological test that would measure any degree of depression. The news he had to give me was not good. The test indicated I was so depressed that the portion of the test showing suicide level went off the scale! I was shocked. I am a Christian, how can I be so depressed? I knew I would never even think of committing suicide. This test couldn't be right.

People who knew me considered me a happy person, upbeat and even funny. I like making people laugh. I didn't feel sad, I just felt tired. I felt so very tired, though, that I had to admit that although I wouldn't ever try to kill myself, I really didn't care if I lived or died. I honestly did not feel the strength to go on. I spent a year and a half at $80 - $100 per hour going into matters of my childhood with my psychiatrist and went on medication also. I did begin to understand things better and did see that I was so out of touch with my feelings and emotions that they had manifested themselves physically in me. I had struggled so hard to suppress them, I guess, that I finally became exhausted.

I accepted by doctor's counsel and changed my co-dependent behavior; then tried to get on with my life, but the symptoms never all went away. There was still a piece of the puzzle missing so to speak, and I didn't know what it was. I asked the Lord to show me through a counselor and made some appointments with Evelyn. The Lord gave her a word of knowledge for me, and it was as if the light came on. I saw a lie that Satan had been using to deceive me most of my life and it was so well hidden and unrecognizable that I had not seen it even when the psychiatrist questioned me about it. I saw the truth, confessed and repented of the resulting sin in my life...Jesus set me free. I felt wonderful!

Evelyn suggested that I go to the next Breakthrough Seminar. I thought to myself, what for? I had already found the answer. I already had my breakthrough. Words cannot describe the wonderful freedom I felt and the joy inmy heart. I didn't think I needed anything else, but God had even more good things in store for me. I did go to the seminar and learned so much. I learned how to do a spiritual housecleaning in my heart so I could keep the freedom God had given me. I learned prayers of protection over my family, myself and even my mind. As I said the prayer of protection the voices of shame, condemnation, accusations and self-hate left me. These voices had been with me since I was a child, making me self-conscious and miserable. I had struggled daily telling myself God loved me over and over, trying to drown out the voices. Sometimes they were louder and stronger than my reasoning's about God's love and I had accepted the lies as truth, but praise God they are gone and the only voice I hear is the Spirit of God within me. If that were not all enough, there is even more. At the end of the seminar as Evelyn anointed us with oil and prayed for us, God healed me of an incurable, untreatable bone disease. I did not expect it, but I felt a bubbling sensation in the affected bone and as I stood and walked, all the heaviness and stiffness was gone. God is so good, He wants to bring us to that place of freedom and the breakthrough is just the beginning.

Jackie Rice

March 18, 1991

Rev. Ted Roberts
East Hill Church
701 N. Main Street
Gresham, OR 97030

Dear Reverend Roberts:
I recently had the privilege of attending a seminar sponsored by your church, conducted by Evelyn Diment. I consider it one of the most meaningful seminars I have had in the last 25 years.

The substance and the spiritual feast that it provided was a major input to my spiritual life.
In addition to it being a spiritual feast, it was like a wholesale cleaning and dealing with my inner life and I want you to know how much I appreciate your ministry, and hers, in providing such a service as this to the community.
I attend church occasionally on Sunday evenings and can see that your ministry throughout the church is a major input to the total community.
In any event, I want you to pass along a compliment to Evelyn Diment for the major contribution that she is doing for your church.
I noticed that the Holy Spirit was in great movement through that time. In fact, the Holy Spirit was the teacher and that was, undoubtedly, the reason it was so outstanding.

There was also about ten healings or more that took place at that particular seminar.

Thank you for your ministering to me.

Sincerely

Robert Briggs

I'm special.
In all the world there's nobody like me.
Since the beginning of time, there has never been another person like me.
Nobody has my smile, nobody has my eyes, my nose, my hair,
my hands, my voice.
I'm special

No one can be found who has my handwriting.
Nobody anywhere has my taste for food or music or art.
No one sees things just as I do.
In all of time there's been no one who laughs like me, no one who cries like me.
And what makes me laugh and cry will never provoke identical laughter
and tears from anybody else, ever.
No one reacts to any situation just as I would react,
I'm special

I'm the only one in all of creation who has my set of abilities.
Oh, there will always be somebody who is better at one of the things
I'm good at, but no one in the universe can reach the quality of my
combination of talents, ideas, abilities and feelings.
Like a room full of musical instruments, some may excel alone,
but none can match the symphony sound when all are played together.
I'm a symphony.
Through all of eternity no one will ever look, talk, walk, think or do like me.
I'm special

I'm rare.
And, in all rarity there is great value.
Because of my great rare value, I need not attempt to imitate others.
I will accept - yes, celebrate - my differences.
I'm Special

And I'm beginning to realize it's no accident that I'm special.
I'm beginning to see that God made me special for a very special purpose.
He must have a job for me that no one else can do as well as I.
Out of all the billions of applicants, only one is qualified,
only one has the right combination of what it takes.

That one is me.
Because...I'm Special

Bibliography and Excerpts from:

Spiritual Warfare As I See It, by Mary Garrison
Healing the Wounded Spirit, by John and Paula Sanford
Seductions Exposed, by Gary Greenwald

Made in the USA
Columbia, SC
21 September 2017